creative ESSENTIALS

David Carter

PLAYS
...and How to Produce Them

with

Illustrations by
Sharman Horwood

and

Computer graphics by
John Arrowsmith

creative ESSENTIALS

First published in 2009 by Kamera Books
PO Box 394, Harpenden, Herts, AL5 1XJ
www.kamerabooks.com

Copyright © David Carter, 2009
Series Editor: Hannah Patterson

ISBN-13: 978-1-84243-220-4

Typeset by Ellipsis Books Limited, Glasgow
Printed by J.H.Haynes Ltd., Sparkford, Somerset

For Hazel,
my first leading lady

ACKNOWLEDGEMENTS

Special thanks are due to all those in the field of amateur drama production who have answered my questions with patience and especially to many members, past and present, of the Southampton University Players, with whom I worked both as actor and director over many rewarding years. The book has benefited from extensive contributions by two old friends, Anthony Pratt, on sponsorship, and Allegra Carlton, on costume, and it has gained in clarity by the illustrations of Sharman Horwood, who worked wonders with my rough sketches, and by the two computer graphics contributed by John Arrowsmith. As ever a great debt of gratitude is owed to my editors Hannah Patterson and Anne Hudson.

CONTENTS

INTRODUCTION

More than a handbook, more than a manual, and more, certainly, than a personal memoir, the present book is perhaps best described as a reflective guide through the make-believe world of play-making, that temporary world filled with temporary people, which somehow manages to live on vividly in the memories and imaginations of those who have taken part in it and those who have seen it.

I have attempted to evoke the entire process of putting on a play with a group of amateur enthusiasts, from the very first daydream about its feasibility through to those small hours at the end of the last-night party. Along the way all the crucial tasks and responsibilities involved in any play production are introduced and explained: setting up a drama group, selecting a director and play, auditioning and casting, designing a set, organising costume and props, and planning lighting and sound. Then there are the rehearsals, tiring but rewarding; the necessary frustrations of the technical and dress rehearsals; and finally the heady excitement of the first night, the ups and downs of the run, and the bittersweet quality of the final performance.

While working on the book it became obvious that there are many aspects of amateur drama production that are scarcely touched on in most manuals of production technique. Most, for example, assume the availability of standard theatre venues. I have at all times, therefore, considered the likelihood that some groups may have to perform in locations which have only the most basic facilities. Thus, while the technicalities of rigging, lighting and sound are explained in simple terms, alternative procedures are suggested for contexts where they may be necessary. Some general advice is also provided on producing plays in the open air, in schools, with non-native speakers of English and expatriates, and also on dealing with the work of playwrights who present special challenges. Methods of creating plays without the use of a script are also explained.

Finally, the 'Resources' section provides information on many organisations, companies, books, manuals and handbooks which provide useful further information on the main areas covered, with some guidelines also for those involved in amateur drama who are considering entering the professional theatre. Please visit www.kamerabooks.com/downloads to access various templates for documents and questionnaires which can be downloaded and used in the organisation of a production.

To make sure that we are all speaking the same language from the start, some illustrations are provided, explaining the terminology used when describing the most common kind of theatrical space: the proscenium arch stage. It should also be remembered that 'right' and 'left' are always from the actor's point of view.

Readers who are also keen to hone their acting skills are recommended to read a companion volume in the Creative Essentials series by the same author, entitled *The Art of Acting. . . And How to Master It*.

It only remains to encourage all those who, after reading this book, plan to undertake their own production of a play, and to wish them every success in the time-honoured thespian manner: 'Break a leg!'

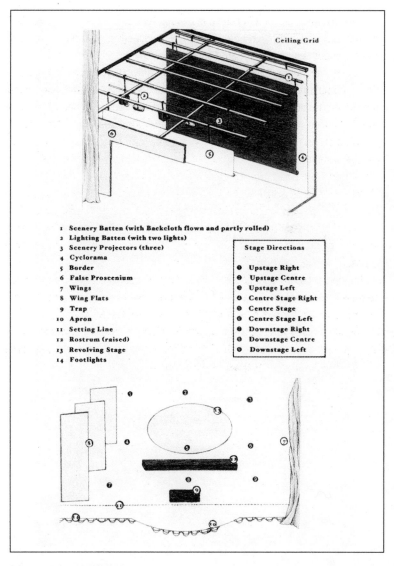

1 Scenery Batten (with Backcloth flown and partly rolled)
2 Lighting Batten (with two lights)
3 Scenery Projectors (three)
4 Cyclorama
5 Border
6 False Proscenium
7 Wings
8 Wing Flats
9 Trap
10 Apron
11 Setting Line
12 Rostrum (raised)
13 Revolving Stage
14 Footlights

Stage Directions

❶ Upstage Right
❷ Upstage Centre
❸ Upstage Left
❹ Centre Stage Right
❺ Centre Stage
❻ Centre Stage Left
❼ Downstage Right
❽ Downstage Centre
❾ Downstage Left

Figure 1. Cutaway backstage view of proscenium arch stage (above) and stage surface with stage directions (below).

1. GETTING GOING

STARTING A DRAMA GROUP

What kind of drama group you set up and how you set it up depends upon a multitude of factors. It is best, therefore, to sit down with a number of like-minded enthusiasts and brainstorm about what you really want to achieve, before even taking the first steps in getting a group together. For the brainstorming, a small, informal group of friends is better than a large group, or you will never agree: with a large group you are likely to spend fruitless hours trying to please everybody, to be all things to all people, and probably become overly ambitious. There are many good arguments for democracy in artistic productions, but there are also times when the Gordian knot has to be cut and decisions made. Hence there is the necessity in virtually all kinds of dramatic productions for a director to provide cohesive form and a vision for the whole. Having someone who is likely to be one of your directors in at the start, therefore, during the setting up of the group, is a good move, if such a person is available at that stage.

The aim of the initial brainstorming should be to produce some kind of programme, a list of aims, a 'mission statement', which can be put boldly and confidently to potential members in your advertising for the group.

There are, of course, some decisions which cannot be made until the capabilities and interests of the group have been assessed. But you should have some concrete proposals at least to discuss with prospective members, and be reasonably sure of the practical arrangements for rehearsals and performances. Otherwise initial enthusiasm will wane rapidly.

First and foremost, information has to be gathered about what facilities (rehearsal spaces, performance areas, etc) are available and whether they can be used by your group, be it free or at a cost. This really is a matter of high priority, because it will define and possibly limit your choice of plays and the general scope of any production.

Performance venues

The first consideration should be the performance venue, because one can afford to be flexible about requirements for rehearsal space (scaling the whole production down if necessary, or making do with a square space instead of a rectangle).

If the group is in the process of being set up, you and a few like-minded friends will have to do some ringing around to possible local performance venues: churches with halls, schools and colleges, pubs with performance areas, hotels with reception rooms, community centres, arts centres – any organisation, in fact, with a hall and/or meeting rooms. Some established theatre groups with their own facilities may also be able to take you under their wing. The use of such venues may or may not have to be paid for; it will depend on circumstances and the generosity of individuals. If your group is located in a small village, your choices may be more limited, but, on the other hand, you are more likely to encounter good will and support among the community.

Once you have a found a venue that is available, looks attractive and seems to fit your general requirements, it must be checked for certain facilities and any limiting conditions:

- Lighting arrangements (Over the stage and in the auditorium? Is there a lighting control box? Can you bring in your own equipment?)
- Sound equipment (Is there a sound system installed? Where are the speakers? Is there a sound control box? Is it near the lighting control box? Can you bring in your own equipment?)
- Power points (Precise locations? Near or on the stage? In the auditorium?)
- Curtain (Drop or drawn apart? Is there one at all? Can you fix one up?)

- Access to the stage (Side and/or back? From the auditorium? Room for shifting scenery?)
- Dressing room/space (Adequate size? Separate for men and women? Washing facilities? Access to toilets? Access to the stage?)
- Storage space (Enough room for scenery, furniture and props? Can items be left there between performances? How easily can you gain access? At all times or only during performances? Can it be locked securely?)
- Auditorium (What is its capacity? How is the seating arranged? Is it fixed or movable? Is the floor flat or raked? Are there aisles? Where are the entrances and exits? How can they be controlled before and during the performance? Is there easy access to toilets? Are there windows and can they be blacked out? Is there a bar or refreshment counter, and who will take the profits? Or are you allowed to provide one? Don't forget to check the current legal requirements relating to the sale of alcoholic beverages.)
- Safety and security (What are the fire precautions and regulations for the building? Where are the fire escapes? Do they function well? Check both backstage and in the auditorium. What arrangements are there for opening up and locking the building? Who has responsibility? Is it safe to leave personal possessions overnight?)
- Availability (Can the venue be available for the dates you prefer? Can it be available for technical and dress rehearsals? And for any other rehearsals? From what time and until what time can you use it? Allow at least one hour either side of a performance, and longer if possible.)
- Cost (Are there any rental fees? Any extra charges? Any hidden costs?)
- Written agreement (Is there a document to sign? If not, it might be wise to compose one specifying all important requirements and obligations after settling all the details, signed by a group member and the person responsible for letting you use the venue. Signed copies should go to both parties.)

Rehearsal space

Yours might be one of those lucky groups allowed to use the performance venue for rehearsals too, in which case most of the concerns in this section will not be relevant. Such good fortune is rare, however (the classic case would be a village group using a church hall). While a good venue is crucial to a good performance, inadequate rehearsal space can mean that, although the performance will certainly take place, it is unlikely to be good. Most amateur groups cannot hope to find more than an adequate rehearsal space, and hopes should not therefore be raised too high. It is unlikely, in fact, that a space will be found which corresponds precisely in shape to the eventual performance space. There is, however, a bottom line, a few basic requirements without which rehearsals will become very difficult.

The area should be, albeit roughly, as close an equivalent as possible to the area of the final performance space. You can lop off a bit here and there – a foot or two, a yard or so – but then you must always keep in the back of your mind, whatever your role in the production – actor, director or crew – that you are only working in a scaled-down version of the final space. It is debatable whether a space that is slightly smaller than desired or slightly larger is to be preferred, but most amateur groups are unlikely to have much choice in the matter. If it will have to serve for a variety of types of production, then a larger space will obviously be more adaptable, and will enable the marking out of a fairly precise equivalent area on the floor. A scaled-down space will mean constantly bearing in mind that distances to be covered on the final set will be longer and must be allowed for. If an actor has to stride across the set while speaking and punch someone on the nose on a particular word, the distance will be all important. (Better to take a specific number of small steps in rehearsal which can be expanded to strides in performance!)

The rehearsal space does not have to be completely empty to start with. Such spaces are, in any case, hard to find. A little clutter can be useful. Some chairs and boxes can be used to double as sofas, pieces of furniture and even rocks in outdoor scenes. Even a space that at first appears impossible can often be adapted, provided that one first seeks permission to move things around, and on the understanding that everything will be replaced as it was found at the end of the rehearsal period. For many years I conducted very successful rehearsals in a university professorial lounge, full of sofas, armchairs and coffee tables. We moved all the furniture back to one end, utilising some pieces for our own purposes, and taking care to make a sketch of the original layout.

A little extra space, not part of the acting area, is also useful, where people can wait and relax when they are not 'onstage', and where props and other items, including clothing, can be kept. It should be noted whether there is a handy drinks-dispensing machine or at least a socket for an electric kettle, so that everyone can take refreshment when needed. If all else fails, encourage everybody to bring flasks of hot drinks. These may seem to be trivial matters, but during long, exhausting rehearsals refreshment will be very welcome indeed.

It is also important not to forget certain crucial practical concerns. If you are begging or borrowing space from a local company, institution or other organisation, certain facts and conditions must be checked:

- Are the building and the room open at the times you have reserved it for? If not, how can you gain access? Can you be loaned a key? Under what conditions?
- If you are rehearsing in the evenings or at weekends, will the lighting and heating/air-conditioning be on? If not, can arrangements be made to have them functioning?
- Are there adequate toilet facilities?
- What are the emergency and security procedures? Where are the emergency exits? Who should you contact in case of emergency, and how?
- If the group is given the responsibility of opening up and closing the room and/or the building, make sure that one person is designated to do both, checking that no one is left inside at the end.
- Are there any costs involved? Do not bring this matter up unless the other party does! Usually most organisations are willing to help out free of charge, and you can always tempt them with the offer of free advertising through a mention in your programmes and on posters.

FINANCE

Although they will have to be taken into account very soon, financial concerns are of only secondary concern at the beginning, when you are setting up a group.

First, you should get your enthusiastic, motley group of would-be actors and crew together and present them with your ideas for productions, venues and rehearsal space, with all the supporting evidence you have gleaned. Do not encourage anything too ambitious to start with: a modest production with a simple set, roles for everyone who wants one, and plenty of things for the crew to busy themselves with. Above all, try to keep it cheap, finding a play which is out of copyright if possible. Do not get mired in financial worries and bureaucratic concerns at the start or you will lose many members very quickly. If you happen to know of any likely sources of finance, mention them, but you can reassure everyone that for the first production it will be possible to cover costs by sharing them as initial membership fees among everyone involved. The more people involved, therefore, the cheaper the whole enterprise will be.

There is no need to rush into any decisions about fees and start collecting money too soon; people are likely to be reluctant to part with any hard cash until they perceive that things are really happening. Get everybody involved first, then, once the group has been functioning successfully for a while – but prior to the first production and before any important bills need to be paid – a meeting can be held to decide what should be charged for annual membership. At this initial meeting it is also a good idea to find out if anyone present knows of any individuals or organisations who might be interested in supporting the group financially. This might be easier to arrange if the group is already part of some larger organisation: a drama group organised within a company or educational institution, for example, might well qualify for some financial support from within the organisation.

Any profits from a production should, of course, be put back into the group fund to support future productions.

Once you are up and running and have demonstrated that you are a viable and successful group you can investigate the possibilities for reliable long-term financial support.

Performing rights

Payment for performing rights, or royalties, is a crucial part of any production's budget. It must be stressed that any drama group which attempts to put on a play without paying for performance rights is undertaking an illegal activity. It is not worth trying to get away without paying, because if you are caught out, your whole standing as a legitimate group will be in jeopardy. It is also extremely unfair to the author of the play or his or her heirs. Playwrights obtain little income in any case from their work.

Details of the amount payable can be obtained through the author's agent, whose address is often included at the front of the edition you are using. If it is not there, the publishers should be contacted. The laws concerning copyright are complex, but the publisher or agent can inform you of the legal situation relating to the play in question. They will also be able to tell you whether a production of the play is being planned by any other group in your area, thus enabling you to avoid clashes.

It is possible that the play you are interested in is out of copyright. This is likely to be the case if the play is from the nineteenth century or earlier. Some old foreign plays, however, which have been translated into English more recently, may still be in copyright. If it turns out that the performing rights of the play you wish to perform are too expensive for your budget, it is worthwhile considering something which is out of copyright.

It is wise not to proceed with any aspects of planning the production until the issue of the performing rights has been settled.

Sponsorship

If you want someone to sponsor your group, you have to have something to sponsor: a truism, but it means essentially that you have to be able to present evidence of a promising, if not yet fully flourishing, organisation. No one is going to sponsor dreams and ideals, so you need hard facts presented on paper (preferably well organised and in an attractive file) to convince your would-be sponsor that you are a worthy cause. In all likelihood, you will not attract a sponsor prior to your first production, because, although you may have many high-quality ingredients for your pudding, the proof will only come when it is served up. A sponsor will be impressed to see that you have actually realised your first dream with success. However, it is always worth a try before your first production, especially with a local organisation with a reputation for supporting the arts. In your file of evidence, along with any other pertinent information, should be a list of your members, with descriptions of their abilities and any relevant qualifications, advertising expenditure, details of venues and any rental costs, a full budget for your first production, with expected profits, arrangements for ticket sales, and how you will display the sponsor's name.

For more detailed advice on sponsorship, from the point of view of the sponsor, I have been able to consult someone with considerable experience of sponsoring theatre groups from an executive position within a major UK company. As Director of Corporate Affairs for Allied Domecq, a FTSE 100 company, Anthony Pratt negotiated the UK's largest arts sponsorship ever with the Royal Shakespeare Company, and also at various times arranged sponsorship for leading pub theatres such as the Gate and the Bush, as well as the Chichester Festival Theatre.

SPONSORSHIP... BY ANTHONY PRATT

Amateurs and professionals

There are likely to be more similarities than differences between amateur and professional companies in trying to get sponsorship. The sponsor's objectives are likely to be similar in both cases: exposure for the company's name (corporate reputation, brand or service), association with quality and relevance to corporate priorities (geography, creativity, entertainment, hospitality, good citizenship, etc).

The amateur drama group, however, can make a virtue of its lack of resources by stressing its closer relationship with a local community, etc. A potential sponsor will believe they can get more for less in terms of the transformations which their money will make possible. Sponsors want to know that their money will be well spent and for clear objectives, the more specific the better. Special rewards may in fact be available for the amateur company which is on the way to becoming professional, as this gives the sponsor the opportunity of getting in on the ground floor and being associated with enabling the emergence of a new company (likely to generate public interest).

Evidence sought by a sponsor

- Quality of work, actual or prospective. Will association with the group bring a benefit to the company? Favourable prior reviews and convincing plans may be important in this, as will word of mouth.
- Indications that you are sponsor-minded. Have you thought about the benefits that a sponsor might gain and the means to deliver them? Provide a menu of possibilities, everything from a credit in the programme to the sponsor's name on a production, in association with the theatre or even as part of your group's name. And think about giving a price tag for each. Don't ask for the earth.
- Relevance. Does your group meet corporate objectives, such as local relevance (e.g. the sponsoring company has its head office or a major place of employment in your area)? Does it promote or embody values the company seeks to embody: creativity, youthful image, modernity, etc?
- Opportunities for entertaining. The sponsor will want to have something they can show people. For example, they may want to invite local MPs, the arts minister, customers, suppliers, employees, etc, to performances or related events.
- The quality of the people they will be dealing with. It is important for the decision-maker in the sponsoring company, or their boss, to know and respect the director or other key people in the drama group. This relationship will be important in ensuring that support will continue.

Best approaches

Personal contact, as in life, is a vital part of the process. Identify and exploit the network of connections which the company and its supporters have. This is important in opening the door and gaining attention.

You can try writing in 'cold' and, if what you say happens to press the right buttons, it may work. Time spent on thinking about what those buttons are is important, as, without a relevant and well-expressed offer, there will be nothing to prevent you from joining the many other speculative letters in the sponsor's wastepaper bin.

Choose your moment. Applying two months before the financial year-end when the budget is already committed/spent or when the company has just announced a large loss and multiple redundancies is not likely to be productive.

Try inviting the potential sponsor along to a production, ask them if they see any way in which you might cooperate to your mutual advantage, make suggestions, and demonstrate that not only are you a promising company worth supporting, but that you will be a constructive and flexible partner. Try to understand the business and its objectives: this may give you a better idea of what to suggest and what to avoid.

If you can, arrange a meeting at which you can present your ideas and discuss what you can offer.

Other targets

As well as companies, there are, of course, other important targets, such as local authorities, parish councils, arts organisations and individuals.

Typically, a local authority will have an arts budget to encourage/develop local talent. Association with local schools and colleges may help here.

Contact arts organisations, such as the Arts Council, Arts & Business, etc. Find out how the Arts Council handles grants, and speak to other groups that have secured funding. What are the right buttons to press? Perhaps you need to stress how your group provides help for or is involved with the disabled, or the underprivileged, and how your activity has an educational aspect, ethnic minority aspect, etc. Arts & Business, which has regional subdivisions, puts together business people and arts companies on a voluntary basis. From them you might get business expertise and help (for accounting, marketing, legal aspects, presentation, mentoring, etc) and they may be able to give you a template for a written sponsorship agreement. They also provide good networking opportunities.

Securing sponsorship from individuals is also a growing part of sponsorship. Individuals can be named as patrons, and ranked as gold, silver sponsors, etc, according to their level of support. You can also give them preferential booking facilities, an interval drink in the bar, etc.

Imitating others

Always be prepared to copy. Look in the programmes of other drama groups and speak to them to get clues as to where they have succeeded and why. If a company turns you down, see if you can find out why. Can you improve what you are offering or the way you put it over?

What can you offer?

Before you do anything else, think about the things you can offer: everything from an ad in the programme to the opportunity to sponsor a tour or play midwife at the birth of an exciting new drama group. Without this forethought the probability is that, in a crowded marketplace where need vastly outweighs available funds, you will get nowhere.

ATTRACTING MEMBERS

A basic golden rule: do not reject anyone who shows real interest in joining you. In a drama production there are usually more jobs than people. Everyone can be useful in some way. And that insufferable individual, who believes he/she is God's gift to the art of acting and may well be the greatest ham who ever trod the boards, will probably fit into a perfectly suitable role in one of your plays. There are, after all, people who ham it up in real life, and characters in certain plays that reflect this. And the person who seems quiet, shy and awkward at first meeting may well blossom forth on the stage; and, if not, they could still be ideal in a small role as a quiet, shy, awkward person.

Of course, the most important method of attracting members is to advertise. Advertise! Advertise! Advertise! In all possible ways and in all possible locations. There are budding drama enthusiasts in all walks of life. Often the most unlikely people can reveal a passion and indeed a talent for it.

It is important to stress here that, if your group is being formed under the auspices of a larger organisation (for example, a company or educational institution), certain restrictions on membership may be imposed on you. But in that case the task of advertising for members is likely to be easier, since the net you cast need not be so extensive.

For wider-based groups the initial advertising will naturally involve some cost in both time and money to you and your small group of fellow enthusiasts, and you may not be able to claim it back later, but that is a risk you have to take. There is no need to be excessive in your expenditure. A clear, reasonably sized poster (A4 or A3), with an eye-catching design and the important words printed boldly, will suffice. Be sure to make clear that all kinds of talent is needed: actors and actresses, of course, but also stage crew (carpenters, electricians, etc), stage management, people handy with needle and thread, decorators, musicians, dancers, etc. Contact details – a phone number and email address – for the person coordinating the responses to the ad should naturally be included in a prominent place.

Try to have your posters displayed in all possible locations, and consider especially the following:

• arts centres
• theatres and cinemas
• public libraries
• community centres
• church halls
• public houses
• cafés and restaurants
• windows of corner shops
• supermarkets
• bookstores
• factory and company notice-boards
• schools, colleges and universities
• specialist shops (those specialising in theatrical make-up, costume, etc)
• bookshops (new and second-hand)

Be sure to check with the management before you attempt to stick up your poster. A practical tip: be sure that they let *you* stick it up (have a glue-stick or tape with you); don't just leave it with someone who promises to do it for you as, more often than not, it will end up left on a desk or under a counter. And make some small (B5) copies, as these can be left in piles or used as handouts.

It's a good idea to start the ball rolling with a meeting, which can be advertised on the poster and take place in a relaxing public place that no one will find daunting, such as a café, pub, or local church hall. The meeting should take place quite soon after the initial advertising – no longer than a week or so – or the interest aroused will have died down and people will have forgotten about it. It is also a good idea to continue the advertising for some time afterwards, perhaps with a newly formulated poster to stress that 'new members are *always* welcome'. Apart from posters, you can consider ads in the local press, if you can afford it, and check if any local free magazines and newsletters will let you have space. And don't forget local TV and radio stations: they often have 'What's On' features and may be willing to mention your group free of charge. Finally, word of mouth is important. Tell all your friends and colleagues, and ask them to tell their families and friends. Give them a few handouts if possible.

It is, of course, important to have some information and a few clear plans to present to would-be members when you meet them. They will want to feel that they will be getting involved in an actual production very soon and not just spending their time discussing and planning. In this way the group will be perceived to be vibrant by all concerned, and will, if it is nurtured well, continue to be vibrant.

A good name for the group is very important. If someone comes up with an apt and memorable one early on, stay with it. If, however, as is so often the case, no one can think of a name which sounds just right, leave it till the first, or even second, meeting with all the new members. After dealing with all the main business, you can wind up the proceedings with a brainstorming session for names. It may well be that one of the new members has a brain-wave, and, if the idea comes from them, this will reinforce the feeling that the group really is all-inclusive.

ORGANISATION

Needless to say, your drama group will need the basic kind of organisation common to any amateur society as soon as a reasonable number of members have been gathered together. A standing committee comprising a chairperson, membership secretary, treasurer and general secretary would usually be the minimum you could get away with.

The chairperson must be a highly motivated person with the interests of the group at heart, and with the force of personality to motivate everyone, and get people to do things, as well as chairing all meetings and being the spokesperson for the society in any negotiations with outside bodies.

The membership secretary must keep a list of all members, with notes on their skills, abilities and interests, contact details, availability, any special considerations (disabled, needs to get home early, etc), and, of course, pursue people to make sure that they pay their membership dues regularly.

The treasurer's job is to keep track of all expenditure and income and deal with sponsors and other financial backers. For important meetings with backers it is useful to have both treasurer and chairperson present. For everyone's peace of mind, regular financial reports and the checking of accounts is to be recommended.

As for the general secretary, he/she will take on all the other odd jobs: writing and posting letters, writing to publishers concerning royalties, taking minutes, organising reservation of venues, etc.

These four positions should be sufficient for the daily running of the society. As the amount of work increases, however, it may become necessary to create more specialised posts, such as a general publicity secretary. It is common, in any case, to have a publicity assistant appointed for each production, so that all publicity for that production can be well coordinated.

While it is often the case that the standing committee will organise and run every activity of the society, there are good arguments for setting up a special committee for the running of each specific production. This would be responsible to the standing committee but should not have to answer for every little decision it makes in the process of pursuing its artistic goals, just so long as it stays within the bounds of the budget. Such a special committee would consist of the director of the play and the main members of the crew. A drawback to this, however, is that it complicates the organisa-tion of the society. In my personal experience, an augmented version of the standing committee, with additional members co-opted for the duration of a production, works very well. One need only add to the basic committee the following: the director, director's assistant, stage manager and publicity assistant. In fact, one might not need the presence of the membership secretary and treasurer at such times.

How democratically the whole operation is to be run will depend as much on production requirements as moral principles, and with most amateur groups it is most often a matter of who is willing or can be cajoled into doing something.

In choosing people for specific offices it is, of course, desirable for individuals to have had some relevant experience, such as secretarial work or management of finances. But general organisational skills and enthusiasm count most. Sometimes you may be lucky to find a single person who will volunteer! So a feeling that someone is reliable and trustworthy is probably the most that you can hope for. In one society of which I was chairman, a shy, retiring lady, who was terrified by the thought of appearing onstage herself, served us devotedly and very efficiently as general secretary for many decades.

CHOOSING A DIRECTOR

I hesitated for some time over whether to place the section on 'Choosing a Director' before that on 'Choosing a Play', or vice versa. My own preference is always for the director to be chosen first so that he/she can suggest a play for the standing committee as a whole to consider and agree on (or not). In this way you can be sure of having a director who is enthusiastic about the production.

With a small group of inexperienced people there may be only one or two individuals willing to take on the responsibility of directing. In fact you may be faced with the possibility of no one being really willing. If there is no clear candidate, then some discreet enquiries should yield the names of possible candidates. Teachers of English in local schools, colleges or universities are likely to be tempted. Apart from the likelihood that they will have an interest in drama, they should have the necessary skills to organise and control large groups of people. It is not usually a major problem to find someone eventually.

If you are lucky enough to be spoilt for choice, promise everyone a chance in due course. Usually availability at the dates and times preferred will help to decide who goes first.

It is also useful and necessary to find out about a director's pre-history, not only with regard to any experience of directing, but also of acting, or working on a show in some other capacity. If there is any uncertainty about their competency, though no doubting their enthusiasm and practical sense, opt for a low-risk production as a first venture: one with few actors, a simple set and little or no technical problems. Unless your director arrives with a set of references and photographs of previous productions, there will always be an element of risk in going for an unfamiliar director. If there are other amateur groups in your area with whom you have good relationships, it may well be that someone who has directed for them but is not currently involved in a production will be willing to direct for you. But this all depends on personal relationships. Some groups might be very possessive about their membership, others less so. In an area where I was chairman of a drama group for a time, all the local drama groups got on very well with each other and would help each other out by sharing not only directors, but also actors, props and costumes when the need arose. With directors and actors there was always the condition, of course, that allegiance was owed first to the group of which one was a regular member.

One amateur group with which I am familiar prefers to select its directors by making them demonstrate how they would stage and direct a scene chosen by the standing committee. This is a rather unreal situation, with the director working in complete isolation from the concerns of a real production, in which a scene must always be understood as a small part of a complex whole. Selection based on such a process will be unreliable as a guide to how a director will work with actors in a real production. Far better to take a calculated risk and observe the early stages of a production closely to ensure that all is running well. As in all working relationships, mutual trust is conducive to the most successful outcomes.

CHOOSING A PLAY

How do you choose? By committee vote? By the votes of all members? By asking the director what he/she wants to do? Or by some combination of these methods? I have indicated already that I believe it is best to let the director suggest a play that he/she would like to do and then agree on it with the whole or a majority of the standing committee. You will probably never get agreement if you attempt to consult all members of the society, some of whom may not in any case feel competent to judge, and feel they are being forced to vote one way or the other.

What kind of play?

While I believe it is important to allow the director artistic freedom in choosing a play, it may be necessary to limit the choice in terms of the kind of play selected. The parameters for selection within which the director can operate may vary from production to production according to the circumstances and competence of the group. Choice may be restricted, for example, because of financial concerns, limited performance area, small membership and likely audience interest. It can be useful to have a general checklist which can be used for each proposed play, with room for notes and comments. The following considerations should be included, with room for extra categories specific to any one play and/or the drama group. The considerations are listed in no particular order, but obviously technical concerns are often paramount. Some concerns may be more important for certain groups than others.

- Technical demands of the play (the nature of the set, special effects, changes of scene, etc). How can they be fulfilled within the limitations of your venue? Are there alternative and easier ways of fulfilling these demands? Can any of them be omitted without compromising the integrity of the play?
- Lighting. Does the play require complex lighting, or can a simple scheme be effective? Apart from the sources of illumination of the set which are kept out of the audience's sight lines, is there any complicated lighting required on the set itself (e.g. flashing neon signs, table and standard lamps, etc)? Is it necessary to have any special lighting effects (e.g. strobe lighting, effect of revolving light from a lighthouse, lights from passing traffic, etc)?

- Sound. Are there any special sound effects? Any disembodied voices? Any offstage noises of a regular or constant nature (e.g. music from a party, crowd noises, passing traffic, etc)?

- Music. Any pre-recorded instrumental music needed for a character to mime a performance to (e.g. a piano, violin, etc)? Any offstage music? Any live music needed onstage (e.g. gypsy band in a restaurant, etc)? If there are songs in the play, how will the accompaniment be provided? Pre-recorded, live onstage, live in an orchestra pit, or elsewhere? You should of course check with the relevant music publishing companies and recording companies concerning performance rights. There may be little or nothing to pay, but it is advisable to be sure.

- Roles. Number of men, and number of women? Any children? Ages of all the characters? Age range? Does anyone have to age considerably in the course of the play? Any linguistic difficulties, such as accents, passages in foreign languages, lisps, etc? Any visible racial distinctions between characters (e.g. a Chinese, Indian, African)?

- How big is the cast? If necessary, is it possible for some actors to double in other roles?

- Length of play. Is it too long, or too short? Will it finish too late for most of the audience, or will it take up barely an hour? How many acts? One, two, three, four or five? Can an interval be fitted in conveniently?

- Genre. Is it a genre your group will enjoy performing and will it attract local audiences? Comedy, thriller, comedy-thriller? Whodunit? Historical costume drama? Melodrama? Period style (e.g. Restoration comedy)? Tragedy? Social realism? Shakespeare or other classic author? Experimental?

- Has the play been performed within your audience catchment area in the last few years, either by an amateur group or by professionals? If it was done very recently it might affect ticket sales. However, people who go to see amateur productions do not necessarily go to see so many professional ones, and vice versa. If it is an extremely popular play, such as a hilarious and well-known farce (by Feydeau, Ayckbourn, Frayn, etc), people may want to see it again in any case, and indeed recommend it to friends.

- Has the play been performed in the West End of London, or any other large cultural centre recently? It may be that people who could not get to see it there will welcome the chance of seeing a local production.
- Costume. Will it require specific period costume? Any difficult costume requirements (e.g. Russian army uniforms, Roman armour, royal regalia, etc)? Can it be done in modern dress?
- Any offensive material? Any aspects of the play which may offend some people's taste or religious convictions? Any bad language? Any sexual innuendo or explicit sex scenes? Any other aspects that might make the production unsuitable for children? You may still want to consider such plays for performance, but need to think about how you will deal with such issues. (Check that nothing you are doing contravenes the law!)
- Is the text of the play readily available? In print, or out of print? In or out of copyright? To whom are any royalties due and how much?

There are publications available to help with the selection of plays for performance. Most notable among them is *The Guide to Selecting Plays*, available in regularly updated editions from a company specialising in theatre books and play texts: Samuel French Ltd (see also the bibliography in the 'Resources' section). This guide is also supplemented regularly by newsletters sent to everyone on the company's mailing list. The *Guide* has a wealth of useful general advice about licences and copyright restrictions, etc. It also has many indexes organised along different lines, so that it is possible to search for plays fulfilling very specific criteria.

First of all, there are the broader categories: full-length plays, one-act plays, revue sketches; plays for children and young people; pantomimes and Christmas plays; musical plays. Within these are numerous other indexes breaking things down even further: by number of characters; number of males and females; and by specific topics and time periods (such as melodramas, Arthurian, First World War, hospitals, ghosts, etc). Useful summaries and comments are provided and the plays can also be traced by title and author. French's *Guide* also contains regularly updated advice concerning copyright laws pertaining to public performances, distinctions between public and private performances, the legal situation concerning charity performances and performances overseas, and advice on rights related to video recording. In all cases concerning legal rights it is crucial to seek permission prior to performance and/or recording.

AUDITIONS

The popular image of an audition is of a stern director seated at an almost bare desk, with notebook and script, under a bright, down-turned lamp, his or her face invisible in the shadows, and a few whispering advisers at hand. A nervous individual in a narrow spotlight on a bare stage recites a set piece, and a voice booms out from the darkness with one of a few stock phrases: 'Next!', 'We'll let you know' or 'Don't call us; we'll call you!'. But auditions do not have to be so daunting.

Even if everyone is completely unknown to each other, it is still not necessary to undergo the stressful process of reciting set pieces unrelated to any play that is likely to be performed. A more convenient method is to have hopefuls read for specific roles in the play one hopes to produce. One can choose sequences or whole scenes and have several actors auditioning together, and then do it again with different actors in the parts or with the same actors playing different roles. In this way the director can get a good idea which actors both sound and look right. It is, however, a little unfair on the actors, who may not yet know much about the play, or even have read it (they cannot be expected to have ordered a copy of the play if there is no certainty of them getting a role).

A far better method for amateur groups, because it also provides an enjoyable social occasion for all the company, is to hold a read-through of the entire play. Light refreshments can be brought along and an 'interval' arranged somewhere half-way. The director can ask individuals to read certain roles, and the casting can be changed completely at the end of every scene, to give everyone a chance to read. It is also a chance for those members of the group who are not actors, or are nervous of acting, to experience taking part in a non-threatening situation. Occasionally one can also invite actors to choose a role they would like to have a go at. The director may feel they are not right for it, but an actor can sometimes surprise you and it is good to give everybody a chance to extend their range. Such an event may be sufficient to enable the director to cast the play, but if it is not, it is always possible to arrange a few extra auditions with selected people, to try out some combinations again, or see people who were unable to come to the reading.

If, after this, there are still a few roles for which no likely interpreters have emerged, you will need to look around and cast your net wider: the right people can come to you via the most unexpected routes. I once found a suitable actor while chatting to someone in a queue at the bank, and on another occasion the cousin of a friend heard about the play and showed interest. How you judge if a person is right for a role is a difficult and challenging task.

CASTING

There is no way round it: the director must know the play and the characters inside out before working on the casting. With an amateur group one cannot hope for ideal casting, and one often has to interpret a character quite freely in order to find someone to play it. With some plays it may be necessary to have someone in mind for the leading roles before casting the whole play. If several powerful performances are called for, you must be sure of having reasonably strong actors available.

The big difference between casting for a professional production and for an amateur one is that the director of a professional production can seek the precise qualities needed in an actor, but for an amateur production you have to make the best of the talent available. This means that you often have to cut corners. A play I was once directing called for a tall, corpulent man who was somewhat simple-minded. There was one actor who could convey the sense of simple-mindedness very well, but he was of average height and build. It would have been very difficult to pad him out convincingly and impossible to stretch his height. Since these physical attributes were not really essential to the character, I decided to omit any references to them in the text. The actor gave an excellent performance in the role.

Basically, as one cannot hope to find many exact similarities between actor and role, one has to look out for 'correspondences': something in the personality of the actor which corresponds with something in the character. It may be only a small thing, such as a tone of voice, a way of looking or moving, or an aspect of personality, such as shyness, impatience, an obsession of some kind. It is not always necessary to tell the actor about this. In fact, telling him or her could be indiscreet or hurtful, and therefore counter-productive. But the director should be able to help the actor develop and build on that aspect of themselves during rehearsal.

A simple example of this occurred when I was casting for a play requiring a rather fussy and meticulous maid. I sensed that one particular middle-aged actress might do well in the part, because of a general insecurity I sensed in her. Shortly after rehearsals started, however, I became aware that she kept moving her forearms and hands about in distracting ways. I finally discovered a way to help her express the fussy meticulousness of the character and use her arms and hands expressively by giving her something to do with her hands in every scene in which she appeared: it might be mixing flour in a bowl, polishing a piece of silver, or whatever. She turned in a very satisfying performance. The leading character in the same play was a married woman of loose morals whose lover kills her husband. I knew something of the personal life of the actress I chose (though I hasten to add that I am imputing no loose morals to her) and felt that she would have understanding and sympathy for her character.

It is especially difficult for an actor or actress to play a character of a completely different age, or to portray the ageing process during the course of a play. Only a few professionals can manage this convincingly. It is therefore important for the director of an amateur production to cast actors who are as near as possible to the presumed age of the characters. Due again to the limited range of acting talent available, this may on occasions be problematic. You can often get away with actors and actresses playing characters who are within a few years of their own age, even where there is a decade or so's difference. This seems to work most convincingly with actors and actresses between the ages of 30 and 50, or thereabouts, who are playing characters not much older or younger than themselves. Outside of these parameters, however, things become a little tricky. While someone in their early 30s can often get away with playing a 40-year-old, and a person in their 40s can often pass for 50 plus, it is not so convincing when a person in their 20s tries to play a teenager, or a 50-year-old tries to play a 70-year-old. It is not just a question of having good make-up, but also of body language and quality of voice. The best advice must therefore be to avoid such miscasting whenever possible. If most professionals cannot manage it successfully, then there is little hope of amateurs being able to carry it off.

If the play has a large cast and doubling is both desirable and possible (in many Shakespeare plays it is almost unavoidable for most groups), you should choose actors who are able to differentiate clearly between the roles. Otherwise this can lead to some confusion, with the audience wondering if the earlier character is now in disguise, or whether it is really supposed to be a different person. Doubling is therefore most successful when the two characters are utterly different (a shy, poorly dressed person and a noisy braggart, for example). If it is just a matter of people in crowd scenes it hardly matters, as long as the costumes are different.

As a general rule it is unwise to attempt to change your casting after rehearsals have started, swapping actors around or dropping one and bringing in someone new. This creates bad feeling, anger and a general lack of confidence in the enterprise as well as in the director's judgement. It may be that, after several rehearsals, you feel you have made a wrong casting decision, but it is far better to live with it and make do with what you have, attempting to bring out the best in the actor or actress you opted for. If an actor or actress drops out for reasons of their own, that is their privilege, and you will then be obliged to recast. You have a right to be angry and remind them of their responsibility to the cast, if this happens at a late stage in rehearsals. Fortunately, most people behave responsibly in this respect. But accidents and illnesses do occur and a crisis may arise at any time, in which case there is no prescribed behaviour. You will have to search around frantically for a replacement. Once, when directing a Shakespeare play, I had an actor in a leading role break his leg four days before the first night and I finally had to take on the role myself, book in hand, with a youthful wig, because there was nobody else who knew his movements, or could be taught them in the short time available. I was praised for having blended my performance in convincingly, with the air of one who always has his nose in a book of poetry (the play was *All's Well That Ends Well*).

FINDING A CREW

There are certain jobs in every production that have to be covered one way or the other. Who does what will depend on the scale of the production. Doubling may sometimes be necessary.

The process of finding a crew should start from the moment it has been decided to undertake a production. You may have your play well cast, but this will be of little use if you do not have a sufficient number of backstage crew to make it all viable. It is best and most efficient to have one person responsible for each duty, but doubling may be possible if the range of requirements for a play is not exceptional. In some cases it may be necessary to have several people handling one task. Costume and props, for example, can sometimes be managed by one person, if the actors are bringing many of their own items of clothing, but with complex productions you may need two or more people dealing with each of these tasks.

STAGE MANAGEMENT

The stage manager is without doubt one of the most important backstage jobs in any production. All backstage crew are important, but the SM has to coordinate and direct every move, light and sound change, etc, in short every single technical aspect of the production throughout every performance. It is he/she who in effect is 'driving' the show. The SM therefore has to be in at every stage of the production and be informed about every aspect of the performance as it develops in rehearsal. It therefore requires someone with a cool head, a flair for organisation and good interpersonal skills.

It is likely that the responsibilities of the SM will be basically the same for all productions, though it does depend on the scale, the complexity of the technology involved, the design of the venue, etc. With professional productions the responsibilities can be very complex indeed, with the need for a number of assistant SMs to cover all the jobs. Certainly it is likely that he/she will need some assistance whatever the size of the drama group.

The SM will need to be conversant with the director's general concept for the play, the design of the set and to be consulted during the building of the set. He/she will need to know exactly how the performance will be lit, how the sound will be organised, and where all the props are to be set, both on the set itself and on the props table. It is also crucial to become familiar with all the actors' moves, entrances and exits, and how these are timed throughout the performance. It will be at his/her direction that every single set change, lighting and sound cue, actor's entrance, etc, will be activated, by voice through an intercom connected to the lighting and sound box and to the dressing rooms. In the absence or failure of an intercom, assistants must convey the SM's instructions promptly as they are delivered. The SM is also in charge of the get-in and get-out and especially the technical rehearsal, at which he/she basically runs the show, trying out every technical aspect until it runs without hitches. During the actual performances the SM's primary responsibility is to cue or 'call' the show from the prompt position near the front of the stage, and in most theatres this is just stage left of the downstage area.

The book

Perhaps the most important of all the preparations the SM has to undertake is the making of 'the book'. This, sometimes referred to as the 'prompt book', is the copy of the play text which the SM prepares in a special file and which contains all the instructions and cues for every single technical aspect of the performance and whatever other details are necessary for the efficient running of the show. It is the SM's bible.

It can be made up in various ways, most commonly by obtaining a cheap paperback copy of the play with an identical text to that being performed and taking this text apart or by making copies by other means. Each page needs to be either mounted on separate large blank sheets or interleaved with such sheets. The main purpose is to provide a copy of each page, with large areas of blank space on at least three sides of it, on which can be noted all the cues and other instructions for the entire play: it is the dramatic equivalent of the musical conductor's score.

All notes and instructions must be written using standard abbreviations and in clear, legible script, just in case someone else has to take over the SM's job at short notice, or for a short time. In preparing the book it is advisable to make all inscriptions first in pencil, in case changes have to be made later.

A very important task is giving cues to actors and crew in due time, and warnings must also be given *before* the cues are given, so that the actor or crew member can be ready to react exactly on cue. If actors are in their dressing rooms they will need to be warned *five* minutes before their cue, to enable them to get to their entrance point on time. At least several minutes' warning needs to be given for all lighting and sound cues as well. Both the warnings and the cues themselves must be indicated clearly in the book. Slow responses to cues are the mark of a poorly prepared production.

There are also specific calls, to actors and crew, which the SM needs to make at certain stages in the performance, and these too need to be marked in the book. These calls start even before the play begins. The 'half-hour call' must be made at exactly *thirty-five* (note the deliberate safety precaution) minutes before curtain-up. Then comes the 'quarter-hour call' at *twenty* minutes before curtain-up, with the 'five-minute call' at *ten* minutes before. The 'final call' is given at exactly *five* minutes before. Then at *one* minute before curtain-up the SM announces 'Places', indicating that everyone should be in their right places for curtain-up.

Included is a sample page from an SM's book (see Figure 2). All cues are given numbers in sequence, so that 'Lx' is a lighting cue followed by its number, and 'Sound Q' is obviously a sound cue followed by its number. The word 'WARN' occurs at the moment in the text when the warning for the next cue is to be given, and 'GO' indicates the exact moment of the cue. The word 'House' refers to the auditorium lights, the word 'tabs' is used to refer to curtains, if they are being used, 'FOH' is 'front of house', i.e. the lobby area of the theatre, and 'pre-set' refers to the condition of the lighting of the set prior to curtain-up (some lighting is often necessary for actors to find their positions, etc). If necessary, numerical and literal references can be used to identify items on the set, such as doors or chairs, to avoid the necessity of long notes, e.g. C1 (chair number one), C2 (chair number two), D1 (door number one), D2 (door number two), T1 (table number one), etc. You can

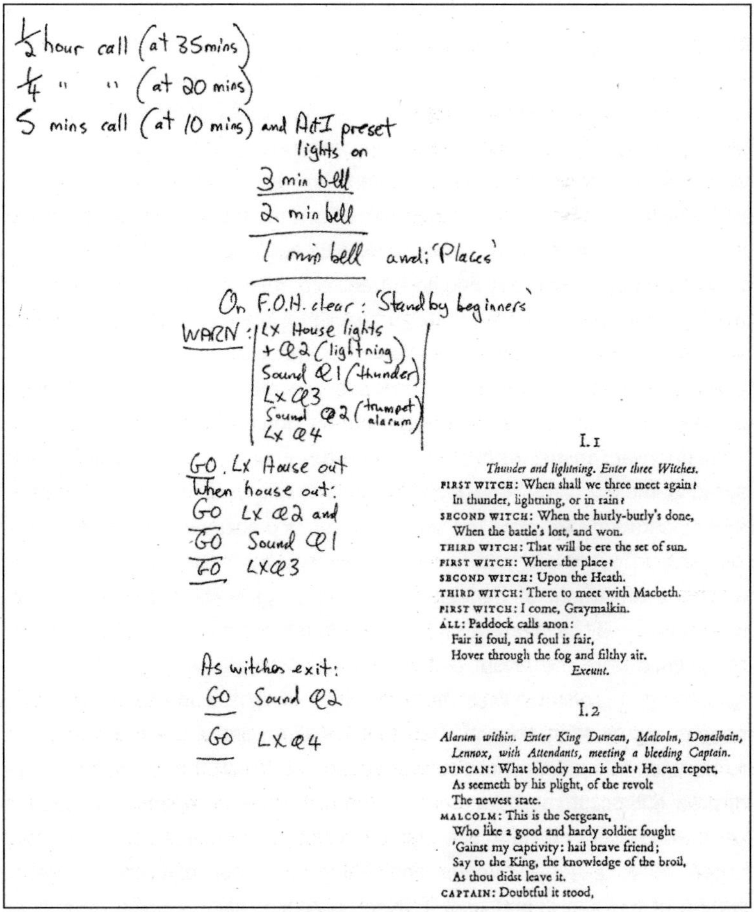

½ hour call (at 35mins)
¼ " " (at 20 mins)
5 mins call (at 10 mins) and Act I preset lights on
3 min bell
2 min bell
1 min bell and: 'Places'
On F.O.H. clear: 'Stand by beginners'
WARN: LX House lights
+ Q2 (lightning)
Sound Q1 (thunder)
LX Q3
Sound Q2 (trumpet alarum)
LX Q4
GO. LX House out
When house out:
GO LX Q2 and
GO Sound Q1
GO LXQ3
As witches exit:
GO Sound Q2
GO LX Q4

I.1

Thunder and lightning. Enter three Witches.

FIRST WITCH: When shall we three meet again?
In thunder, lightning, or in rain?
SECOND WITCH: When the hurly-burly's done,
When the battle's lost, and won.
THIRD WITCH: That will be ere the set of sun.
FIRST WITCH: Where the place?
SECOND WITCH: Upon the Heath.
THIRD WITCH: There to meet with Macbeth.
FIRST WITCH: I come, Graymalkin.
ALL: Paddock calls anon:
Fair is foul, and foul is fair,
Hover through the fog and filthy air.
Exeunt.

I.2

Alarum within. Enter King Duncan, Malcolm, Donalbain, Lennox, with Attendants, meeting a bleeding Captain.

DUNCAN: What bloody man is that? He can report,
As seemeth by his plight, of the revolt
The newest state.
MALCOLM: This is the Sergeant,
Who like a good and hardy soldier fought
'Gainst my captivity: hail brave friend;
Say to the King, the knowledge of the broil,
As thou didst leave it.
CAPTAIN: Doubtful it stood,

Figure 2. 'The book'.

also distinguish items using colour codes, and characters can be indicated by their initials, e.g. M (Macbeth), LM (Lady Macbeth), BG (Banquo's ghost), etc. This is necessary as often the action or words of a character also function as sound, lighting or other technical cues.

Rigging lighting and sound

One demanding and time-consuming but crucial task requiring the presence of the director, stage manager and sound and lighting experts is positioning and adjusting the sound and lighting equipment. This rigging, as it is called, has to be carried out separately for sound and lighting, although in performance they will have to be very closely coordinated. How complex the arrangements are will differ from production to production and from venue to venue. In a reasonably well-equipped theatre it will be an intricate process, needing people of real expertise in their field. The sound and lighting experts will have to go through the entire play from the pre-set stage (before the play starts) to after the final curtain, plotting every single lighting and sound cue in sequence. In modern theatres this can all be fed into a computerised system, so that during the performance it is a straightforward matter of clicking on a cue number. With less sophisticated systems the operators will have to adjust the lighting manually through a switchboard for each cue. The SM's role in this process is central, as he/she will have to cue the sound and lighting during the performance.

The arrangement of the lights, and choice of kinds of lights, including whether they will have any gels (coloured filters), can be judged approximately in advance from the layout of the set and close study of the text for any special lighting effects. Thus the basic array of lights can usually be set up prior to the plotting session, but final tweaking and adjustment will have to be undertaken with the director present, to check that they provide the desired effects. It may also be discovered that an extra light is needed to cover some area of the stage. Then, starting from the pre-set, the lighting expert must take the director and SM through the play checking each setting of the lights, and each cue for changes, also deciding on intensities, fades, etc. When agreed on it is a good idea to run the sequence of a change to check if it is satisfactory. The SM will need to be noting all this down to be included in the book. It is useful to have a willing body present to stand on the stage and take up positions that will be assumed by actors in performance or move pieces of furniture if necessary. This will enable precise focusing. The whole process takes an extremely long time, as each light has to be focused individually for each setting. One should allow double the likely length of the performance, and then some!

Organising the sound equipment and plotting the sound cues will also take a long time for most plays, and will have to be fitted in with the lighting cues, so that the precise sequence is clear, e.g. a lighting cue followed by a sound cue, followed by another lighting cue, or whatever. Despite the fact that, for most productions, the sound cues are not likely to be as compli-cated as the lighting cues, you should bear in mind that it is not only a matter of sound effects per se, but also involves the use of any recorded music, including any background music to be played while the audience is coming into the auditorium, and at the intervals. The precise lengths of the pieces of music need to be calculated (always allowing for more than one thinks will be needed, in case of delays), as do the lengths of the fades, up and down, as well as the volume levels. For sound effects the source of the effect has to be determined: does it come from backstage (left or right) or from the back of the auditorium, etc? All this has to be noted by the SM. Finally, the SM will have to note down clearly in the book every single sound and lighting cue agreed on.

The technical and dress rehearsals

The stage manager is very much in charge of the whole performance from the technical rehearsal onwards. Some drama groups may be able to manage several technical rehearsals and dress rehearsals, as in the profes-sional theatre, but with pressure of time and possibly limited access to the performance venue, the most that amateur groups can usually hope for is one of each. However, this is perfectly adequate if everyone is well-prepared beforehand. (For details of general procedure at both these rehearsals, see the relevant sections later in this book.)

Before the technical rehearsal the SM must check every aspect of the set for safety and to ensure that moving parts, such as doors and windows that have to open, are working properly. Is the set properly dressed? Are all crew in position and are all systems functioning well? If any cue is late or omitted, any crucial movement wrong, any lighting or sound effect late, etc, he/she must stop proceedings and insist that it be gone over again until it is correct. Before any re-run of a sequence the technicians should be told what condition to go back to, e.g. 'Stand by for cue 27', and the actors informed of where in the text they will be running from. It is a frustrating and at times irritating process for all concerned but there is no way round it: every single cue and its changes must be gone through again and again until it is absolutely spot on.

When it comes to the dress rehearsal, which for most groups will be the final rehearsal before the first night, it is to be hoped that everything will run as in the real performance, but if something really crucial goes wrong, the SM must be firm and insist that a sequence be run again. Once the production is in performance mode, there will be no chance to try it again: everyone, including the SM, will just have to soldier on, maintaining the illusion, as convincingly as possible, that all is well.

After the show

When the run is over, the stage manager's job is not yet finished. He/she must oversee the entire get-out (see the relevant section later in this book) and make sure that all safety concerns are respected in the process. Is everyone doing their job in dismantling the set, lights and sound equipment, collecting up costumes, gathering props, etc? Finally, he/she must ensure that all rubbish is removed and disposed of and that the stage and backstage are swept clean, out of courtesy to the management.

Lighting

Theatrical lighting is a science in itself. There are ways, however, to keep it simple and manage with minimal effects. In this section a survey of working possibilities is provided, from basic requirements to optimum effects.

You realise how much you depend on lighting and what you can get away with when there is a power failure. In a winter of union discontent in the UK, I was directing a production of Bertolt Brecht's *Schweyk in the Second World War*. Power cuts were likely and unpredictable. One member of the cast dreamed up a brilliant back-up system, which, fortunately, we only had to bring into action on one night. The emergency lighting proved to be stunning and strangely effective. It added a sharp, expressionist quality, by no means out of place, to our production of the Brecht play. Two flood lamps, one at the back of each of the two aisles in the small theatre, were connected by cables to the batteries in one of the cars belonging to a cast member. Our range of effects was rather limited (they were either on or off), but the play could go on. The situation created a remarkable bond between cast, crew and audience, with everybody willing the system to work. The only person to suffer was the one whose car was used: by the end of the evening his batteries were almost flat and he had to walk home.

The experience with the Brecht production also taught me that good lighting is a luxury and not a necessity. Of course you need lighting, but if you have a well-performed play with an enthusiastic audience, simple lighting is often sufficient, and even rudimentary lighting will work: lights that go on and off over the stage area and another set of lights that go on and off over the audience. I have produced many a good play with students under such conditions. A step up from this would be to have lights over the stage that can be switched between low, medium and high, or can be dimmed and raised again. If their angles can be modified this will be a further boon.

Even if more complex lighting is available, with a range of spotlights and coloured lights, it may not be possible to alter or move them during the performance. Everything may have to be pre-set. The more complex the lighting available, or that you can borrow, or afford to hire or purchase, the more you will definitely need expert advice. Not only will an overenthusiastic amateur fiddling around with lights while following a manual be unlikely to provide the effects the director desires, but the whole enterprise will be dangerous.

All electrical fittings are a serious business, and it would be better to coax the owner of the local electrical goods or repair shop into joining your group, with the promise of free advertising, than to take any risks.

To ensure that you and your lighting expert are speaking the same language, there follow explanations of a few basic concepts and some facts about stage lighting.

Whether you buy or hire lighting equipment, there are four main types of light used in theatrical productions:

Floods

Floodlights provide general overall lighting, especially for lighting scenery and cycloramas.

Beamlights

Beamlights provide an intense but narrow beam of light, and are useful for suggesting a strong shaft of light such as sunlight.

Profile spots

These provide a sharp beam of light which can be precisely controlled using masking and shutters.

Fresnel spots

These are quite versatile lights and provide a softer light than profile spots. The beam can be adjusted by using shutters and by changing the distance between the lamp and the lens. They come in a large range of wattage, with the 250 to 500 watt lamps usually being sufficient for small theatres.

When drawing up plans for the distribution of the lights around the acting area, it is useful to follow the international conventions for representing different kinds of lights, as shown in Figure 3.

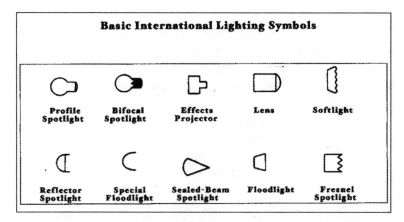

Basic International Lighting Symbols

Profile Spotlight	Bifocal Spotlight	Effects Projector	Lens	Softlight
Reflector Spotlight	Special Floodlight	Sealed-Beam Spotlight	Floodlight	Fresnel Spotlight

Figure 3.

To light a figure onstage well, the angle of the lighting is crucial. It must be steep enough to reduce the shadows falling from the actor onto the set, but low enough to throw sufficient light onto the actor's face. Generally a 45 degree angle is best, as in Figure 4.

Many dramatic effects can be obtained through simple methods. To light a face so that it appears to be lit naturally requires a carefully balanced array of lights (for clear representations of the variations possible see Figure 5).

Coloured lighting is an intricate process and requires knowledge of some basic laws of physics relating to the mixing of coloured light. These are not the same as for coloured paint! If lights with red, blue and green mediums are directed at the same point, the effect will be white light. Remove one of these colours and a blend of the other two will appear. A blue medium transmits blue, blue-green and green, while a yellow medium transmits yellow, red and green light.

Sound

Similar basic principles apply both to lighting and sound. You can keep it extremely simple or make it very complicated. This will depend very much

Angles of Lighting

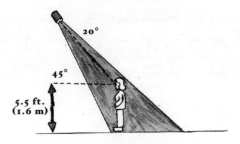

When lighting the actor on stage, one or two beams at a 45° angle are usually used. This angle diminishes the actor's shadows on the set, and yet they are low enough to illuminate the actor's face.

However, when the actor needs to be lit completely, two lights, placed 90° apart, yet still set at a 45° angle, will permit some movement within the lit area on stage.

Figure 4.

on the facilities, the group's budget and the technical expertise available. Keeping it simple should not be regarded as a failure: it can be a distinct advantage. If the whole production is being undertaken with the minimum of technical support, and if it is also being performed in several different venues (taken around to schools or clubs, for example), simplicity is clearly

Lighting: Basic Angles

Normal Light

A side backlight set at the height of the actor, along with a high, side back light, plus a direct front light, will give normal lighting.

Front Light

A front light shines directly on the actor's face and flattens the features.

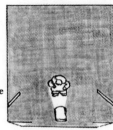

Side Light

Side lighting lights the actor's face when turned towards the wings, and gives it solidity and roundness.

Back Light

A back light gives a halo effect around the actor.

Key Light

Key lighting is the main source of lighting in any scene.

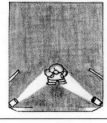

Figure 5.

Top Light

Top lighting can be used for dramatic effect.

Footlights

Footlights can cast shadows and give an eerie effect.

Wings

Cross Light

Cross lighting is used as a horizontal side light.

Fill Lights

These fill in any shadowy areas.

Figure 5. (cont.)

a virtue. I have directed several productions for which we made use of just one good cassette player. It is the quality and clarity of the sound which is especially important. If, however, your stage is wired for a sophisticated sound system, you will clearly have to seek professional advice, and such a venue will be bound to have someone on hand. It might be necessary to have a member of your group instructed in handling the equipment, especially if it involves computerised programming of the sound cues. There is, of course, a whole range of possibilities between the simple use of a cassette player and a completely computerised sound system. The watchword is: don't despair! One way or another you can organise workable sound for your productions, if necessary with a combination of methods.

As with lighting, so with sound: it is advisable to have a back-up system. There should be a Plan B, in case a technical hitch occurs. Simple measures suffice: have a *second* cassette player on hand, plus replacement batteries, in case there is a fault with the wall-socket, etc. Such apparently small considerations can save a whole performance.

If you are using a cassette player, then have each sound item (be it music or sound effect) ready at its starting point on *separate* tapes. It is not advisable to put all the sound items on one cassette, because it is likely to prove difficult to find each cue easily in semi-darkness. Have a box with each sound item on its separate cassette lined up in order in the box, and clearly numbered and labelled. Have duplicates on hand in another box. What would happen if one tape got snarled up?

With recordings on CDs or CD-ROMs, it is obviously much easier to find cues. But it is crucial to try out the system in the lighting conditions which will prevail during a performance. Will the operator be in a little room of their own with good lighting, or hunched behind the curtain with a torch? Again: make duplicate recordings. There is always that one fatal occasion when someone steps on your CD, or you scratch it with a fingernail. And don't forget to have a second CD-player on hand too.

If you can record everything on computer in sequence, and just need to click on a key at the right moment, that will, of course, make the whole process much easier. But experience, not only with play productions but also in giving conference presentations using PowerPoint slide and sound shows, teaches that computers will also let you down at crucial moments. You cannot freeze the whole performance while you desperately try to conjure up that sound of the car arriving! Thus, even with the most up-to-date computerised sound system, it is advisable to have a back-up system using more primitive technology. Even if you never have to use it, you will know it is there in case of emergency. You will be able to proceed confidently in the knowledge that, whatever happens, the show will go on.

Sound effects can be created and obtained in a variety of ways. Many may frown at the use of traditional physical and mechanical effects, but they have the advantage of not being subject to electronic faults, and can be easily operated at will. It is well worth investing in the purchase or construction of such devices as a wind machine, a thunder sheet, a door-slam, etc. There are also many collections of sound effects available on CD and some are also downloadable from websites (see the 'Resources' section). It may be necessary, of course, to record sounds unique to a particular play (a crowd singing a specific song, for example).

Selecting music is a much more straightforward matter than finding sound effects. The director will probably have his/her own ideas about what music, if any, is suitable for background music, to cover scene changes, to set a mood before the curtain goes up, or maintain an atmosphere during the interval, etc. One tip is always to record much more music than you think will be needed. Inevitably, there will be occasional delays in scene changing (someone cannot find a crucial prop, or it takes longer to shift a piece of scenery than usual).

Another practical hint about the use of recorded music is that, unless sudden dramatic chords are required, one should *always* fade it up at the beginning. This could be a slow or fast fade, but always fade one way or the other. Otherwise an irritating click is likely to be heard through the loudspeakers as the equipment is turned on. For the same reason the music should always be faded down at the end before switching off.

Live music brings its own problems and rewards. If it is suitable, live music adds a whole magical dimension to a production. Sometimes it is called for in the script and is an essential part of the action, as with an actor or actress performing at a piano. This will sound much more convincing if it is mimed to a live player at another piano in the wings. There may also be occasional songs incorporated in the play, as with Shakespeare or Brecht. Onstage musical performers can be organised, or a small group situated offstage, perhaps in a corner of the auditorium if no theatrical pit is available. Such live music must be rehearsed thoroughly together with the actors well before the technical rehearsal.

Needless to say, the director, or some other delegated person, should also check that all issues of music performance rights have been settled.

At some point someone, often an inexperienced actor, may well raise the question of whether you will be using microphones in the production. This usually indicates insecurity about strength of voice. Commonly envisaged are either a number of microphones hanging above the stage, which are assumed to be somehow capable of picking up all actors' voices, or body microphones, these being common in TV and film work. I have never used microphones in stage productions, except where the play specifically requires them (at a rally, in a night-club scene, etc). It is far better for the actors to get used to speaking loudly and clearly and projecting their voices.

Costume

While I am fairly well acquainted with the requirements for costume in many types of play, and with the priorities involved in organising it for a production, I am a dab hand with neither needle nor sewing machine, and I don't understand much about the finer points of costume design, making and fitting.

Fortunately a very old friend is skilled in this aspect of amateur drama. Allegra Carlton is a long-standing member of the Southampton University Players, and is very experienced in matters of costume and also as an actress – in addition to being no mean singer! It was natural, therefore, that I should turn to her for advice on costume in preparing this book.

COSTUME... BY ALLEGRA CARLTON

From day one

As the wardrobe supervisor (also frequently known as wardrobe 'master' or 'mistress'), you need to get involved at the design stage of the show. You are an integral part of the production team. If it is a big show, appoint a wardrobe assistant, or even two, and, if it is two, agree at the beginning what each of them is going to do. You will be expected to attend production team meetings; you should also have wardrobe team meetings if you have wardrobe assistants. At an early stage discuss with the director what overall look he/she wishes to have for the show. Some directors will give very general guidelines and be open to suggestions, but others will have a very clear and detailed idea of what the costumes should be, right down to shapes and colours. As you develop your own ideas it is very useful to have photographs available from books or other productions, or sketches to show the director and help him or her visualise what you have in mind.

Checking the text

READ THE SCRIPT! Work out what costumes you think people will need and how many costume changes there will need to be and how quick they will need to be. For very fast costume changes you need to plan in advance how to make this as easy and quick as possible. Can a costume be fastened with such materials as Velcro rather than buttons or hooks and eyes?

Agreeing a budget

It is advisable to agree a budget for costumes in advance, but make sure it is not cast in stone! I have found that budgeting for between £10 and £30 per costume tends to be more or less on the mark, but it does depend enormously on what kind of show you are looking at. If you are going for period, you may have to hire (particularly if you want military uniforms, for instance, or hunting dress) and this can be expensive. If you need to hire proper wigs, these will be really expensive: they are about £100 each per week to hire and have to be very carefully looked after. You will be under pressure to keep costs down as much as you possibly can. You need to be prepared to fight your corner on this, but be realistic: the show has at least to break even for the society to be able to continue.

Doing research

I use the Internet a great deal when researching costumes, especially period costumes. There are lots of wonderful websites showing, for instance, how to tie a Regency cravat, or dress hair, or how to tweak a basic dress shape to get variations on it. There are loads of costume books which are very helpful in giving a basic idea of dress styles for different periods. Unless you are performing for a re-enactment society, you will be more knowledgeable than the audience.

The total look

Wardrobe is not just about clothes. It is about the total look of each actor. It therefore includes hairstyles, hair dressing and wigs, and appropriate jewellery and footwear for the period, not to mention other props such as canes, fans, fobwatches, reticules, pomanders, ruffs or ruffles, etc. It also includes how people sit, stand and move about, so the wardrobe supervisor may need to coach the cast in this, with the director's agreement. But, having said all this, costumes can be very simple and still be incredibly effective.

Taking measurements

As early as you can during rehearsals, make a list of every member of the cast and take their measurements. DO NOT take their word for their measurements, although you can ask women what dress size they usually buy, and be very firm about getting up-to-date ones. Do not rely on last year's measurements unless you know for a fact that nothing has changed. I find it helpful to take the following measurements:

- height
- nape of neck to waist to give upper-back length
- waist to floor for women wearing long dresses

- head (if hats are to be worn) from brow around the widest part of the skull at the back of the head
- neck (men) for collar
- across the shoulders
- shoulder to wrist down the outside of a bent arm
- bust or chest measurement
- underbust measurement for women for any closely fitted dresses, e.g. Regency
- waist measurement (Check exactly where the waist is! It is actually just above the navel, but many men believe it is much lower. For modern dress they can get away with this, but for period clothes they cannot.)
- hips for women (about eight inches below the waist)
- inside leg for men
- shoe size
- shoe width

Numbers and lists

How many pieces of clothing comprise each costume and what are the relevant measurements for each piece? For a man's shirt, for example, you might only need to record the neck size and the colour you are looking for. If they have two costumes or more, can you cheat on this by just adding a coat, or an apron, or something similar? For each costume, do you need a separate set of accessories, or can you get away with one set?

It is helpful to make a separate list of clothing required for each person, which I tick off as I find each item, but also to list by categories, e.g. 20 shirts, 5 x 15" neck, 8 x 16" neck, etc.

Wigs

If you are hiring proper theatrical wigs, you will be provided with a whole set of measurements needed in order to provide a wig of the correct size. You can get cheap wigs from various costume and fancy-dress shops, but the possibility of re-styling these is extremely limited, so you are confined very much to what the wig looks like, whereas a professional wig can be styled (by the wig provider, not by you) in any style you request. Work out what each character needs.

Hiring costumes

Other local amateur drama groups may be willing to hire out cheaply (and even lend free) costumes from their wardrobes. Your local professional theatre may be prepared to lend or hire out costumes at a relatively cheap rate, and some national companies also hire out costumes, e.g. the National Theatre, the Bristol Old Vic, etc. Some county councils have wardrobes from which they rent out costumes to schools and amateur companies (Hampshire County Council, for one). There are also many private-hire shops and companies. Some local ones just have very basic costumes, while others have a wide range. Yet others offer a specialised selection. Some can be found on the web, some advertise in *Yellow Pages*, and some seem to operate on a word-of-mouth basis. Ask as many people as you can about finding things. Talk to museums, visitor centres that use costumes, re-enactment societies, etc. Especially helpful can be local interactive museums where visitors can dress up in period clothes as part of the experience.

If hiring from a professional theatre, it is important to be aware that the theatre company can override an external hire if they suddenly need the same costumes you have booked. This happened to our drama group once when we had hired some costumes from the Bristol Old Vic.

Normally, if you hire a costume, you *must* undo alterations before returning the costume. It is good practice to check with the hire company what their position is on making slight alterations (e.g. raising or lowering a hem, taking in/letting out) *before* doing any alterations. Some may request that alterations be hand sewn rather than machine sewn, as machining can leave a trace on delicate fabrics. If there is any damage to hired costumes, you will need to do your best to repair it as professionally as possible. If it is really bad damage you will need to discuss it with the hire company and work out what to do.

Some theatre-hire companies will hire out the entire costume, including accessories and shoes. Others will hire out only the individual garments, but may have a stock of accessories for hire.

Making costumes

This is huge fun but can take an inordinate amount of time. Sometimes, however, all you need is a single item to create an illusion. You do not have to use fabrics, but can use plastic, paint, all sorts of stuff.

Work out in advance how many costumes you need to make, and plan the time you are going to need to make them. Check what you already have available. Can you adapt existing costumes rather than make new ones? Don't be a perfectionist. This is drama, not film, so there are no close-ups (unless you are in a small theatre where the audience is within three feet of you), and you can cheat quite a lot. You do not need to finish seams perfectly and a machined hemline is going to upset no one.

Are there any other experienced seamstresses in your group, or among their relatives? Many people have relatives or friends who make clothes or upholstery or curtains. Can you get help with making stuff? Ask around really early and delegate! But make sure that you have agreed exactly what each person is going to do.

It is also very useful when making clothes for a show to have a dressmaker's dummy on hand.

Finding materials

Second-hand curtains from charity shops are wonderful for anything period and are much cheaper than anything else you will find. Duvet covers can also be adapted, but one must watch out for uneven fading (I have made three Regency dresses from duvet covers and they were hugely successful). If there are any big fabric warehouses around then use these. Asian fabric shops, for example, have some wonderful fabrics. You can also use standard dressmaking and curtain shops. You will find after a while that people will be eager to donate to you stuff that they would otherwise throw away, particularly old curtains. Do not accept everything, however, or you will have more than you can cope with.

Shoes

Things like shoes can often be cheated on. Many men have lace-up shoes which can be disguised to look like period shoes: a big cardboard buckle on a black piece of elastic can easily be slipped over a shoe to hide the lace. And you can easily get away with slip-on court shoes or ballet shoes for women in a lot of period plays. It is quite in order to ask all the women in the cast to provide their own small, ballet shoe-style flatties, which they will be able to use again in future productions. Some theatre-hire companies will also hire out shoes together with the costumes.

Fittings

It is important that the costumes are available well in advance of the technical and dress rehearsals. It is useful to allocate and get them tried on at a couple of the final rehearsals, but this needs to be agreed with the director. The cast could arrange to visit you privately for fittings, but this is usually time-consuming for all concerned. Once costumes are allocated, and depending on their value, the cast can be asked to take full responsibility for their own. All costumes need to be complete and allocated before the technical rehearsal, and certainly before the dress rehearsal, for any quick changes to be practised. The earlier actors have their costumes, the better they feel, and many welcome the chance to rehearse in them. It also makes the director feel more secure.

Final rehearsals and performances

Watch the technical and dress rehearsals. You need to check for problems with costumes and the way people are wearing them, so that any problems can be ironed out before the show. At the technical rehearsal allocate dressers for anyone who needs a quick change. You will be one of the dressers yourself but you may need others. Do not expect the stage manager to organise this: it is your responsibility. Make sure that costumes for quick changes are where they need to be. During the show you need to be backstage throughout as a dresser and also to do any running repairs. If you cannot be there, you need to have a wardrobe assistant who can do this for you.

After the show

You need to collect every item and check it off against what was handed out. It can be useful to give each cast member a sack to put their costume in after the last performance. DON'T let the cast take their costumes home for washing unless you are prepared to wait weeks or months for them to get round to returning the cleaned items.

Hired costumes may need to be washed or cleaned, but a lot of hire companies prefer to organise this themselves. If you have had a show in which hired costumes got particularly dirty (e.g. an outdoor show during which there was a lot of rain and the costumes got muddy), discuss this with the company and find out how they wish you to deal with the matter.

Hired costumes will also have a deadline by which they must be returned. Taking longer than this will cost you extra money, so you need to arrange for costume return to be prompt. And when collecting the costumes, do not forget to collect all the accessories too.

Very often costumes just get put back into the wardrobe unwashed. This is fine if the costume has not been heavily worn, but this practice can lead to seriously smelly costumes if they have seen a lot of action. It is therefore worth spending a bit of extra time washing costumes, provided that they are not likely to shrink.

Costume storage

So you have got all these costumes. Now, where are you going to keep them? Are they the kind you can use again or do you just take them along to a charity shop? Does the group have wardrobe space available? If not, can you share wardrobe space with another local group? Is there room in your loft or the loft of another member (and is the floor strong enough)? Wherever you manage to store them, it is a good idea to sort the clothes in the wardrobe by type: trousers together, shirts together, etc. It is useful to make a catalogue of what is in the wardrobe, including sizes. This is easier when starting a wardrobe than when inheriting a fully formed one. It is also useful to go through it every so often chucking stuff out. The key to the whole thing is organisation.

Make-up

It must be stressed from the outset that theatrical make-up is a complex art. Professional actors learn to put on the rudiments themselves, but they still need frequent expert advice and assistance; so it cannot be expected that amateur actors will master the art sufficiently to enable them to apply more complex make-up and develop special effects. It is therefore advisable to have at least one person in the group who is willing to study specialist theatrical make-up books and even obtain some training in the techniques. Often actors can apply the make-up themselves if they are given clear instructions. It is necessary, however, to have one person on hand to advise and instruct: before the technical rehearsal to discuss make-up with every actor and give advice on what will be necessary; then at the dress rehearsal and throughout the run to help in the application of make-up. It may be necessary to have a few assistants working under a make-up supervisor, especially if there is a large cast. At the technical and dress rehearsals it is crucial that the make-up supervisor go out front and wander round the auditorium to observe every actor's make-up. Is it as effective as intended? Is it a little too strong, or too weak? Notes should be made to convey any concerns to each actor during a suitable break in proceedings.

To make-up or not to make-up?

Many of those inexperienced in the theatre assume that make-up is always necessary and very easily go over the top in the application of it. One must always apply what is sufficient to the circumstances, but no more than that. For a production with a small cast in a small theatre, in which the audience is very close to the actors, one usually needs hardly any make-up at all, unless special effects are necessary. Just a little to counteract the reflections of the lights on shiny skin should suffice.

What kind of make-up to apply and how extensively to apply it depends on the basic conditions of auditorium size, the closeness of audience to actors and the strength of the lighting. Strong stage lighting makes the face look generally flat and the skin generally pale. A member of the audience looking at a brightly lit play from a considerable distance will not be able to perceive detail of expression if no make-up is used.

In order to apply make-up correctly, a large mirror at face height will be necessary, preferably as part of a dressing table. If they are not already fitted, some lights should be fixed around the edges of the mirror, so that the face is clearly illuminated from the front.

Straight make-up

For most realistic plays with standard lighting, only what is known as 'straight make-up' will be necessary. This does not look natural from up close, but from a distance appears to be so. The actor's natural features are heightened but not changed in any way. Such make-up must follow the natural lines and features of the face, and not be applied 'against the grain', or the face will take on strange expressions when the actor speaks or even smiles.

Character make-up

Sometimes it is necessary to change the appearance of an actor, but in a naturalistic way. For example, he/she must be made to look younger or older or sick, etc. This is known as 'character make-up'. For these effects, lines, highlights and shading are used. This is where the skill of a trained make-up expert becomes crucial in knowing just how much make-up to apply, what tones to use, etc. Applied wrongly, such make-up can make an actor look positively cadaverous at one extreme, or like some pink-faced doll at the other. It is important that the final effect look convincing as a natural development of the actor's real face when seen on the stage, and not like a wooden mask.

Stylised make-up

Under the heading of stylised make-up can come all other kinds of make-up not intended simply to heighten natural effects. It ranges from period make-up – for Restoration comedy, for example – in which case the fashions of a particular period have to be researched and recreated, to the creation of fantastic make-up for actors imitating animals, wizards, fairies, elves, aliens and the like. Make-up for the latter must not only be well researched but also requires very complex techniques of application, and it is advisable to seek professional help for this. For all such special make-up effects the make-up supervisor must work closely with the director from the start to ensure that the final effects are in harmony with the general look of the production, including set design and colours, as well as with the costumes.

Make-up kit

A fully equipped make-up box, with dividing sections and trays, with all the basic materials needed for the application of standard make-up, should contain the following:

- make-up brushes of various shapes and sizes: including very fine brushes for eye-lining and bushy ones for cheek colouring, etc, with a good range in between
- cotton wool balls and pads, etc
- eyebrow pencils and eyeliners (liquid, cake and pencil)
- mascara
- eye shadow in various colours (and in powder, liquid and cream form)
- false eyelashes
- black tooth enamel
- powder puffs
- foundations (various kinds according to preference: cake, liquid, grease-paint or stick)
- lining colours (pots or sticks)
- face powder
- rouge
- make-up remover
- cleansing cream

In addition, for any special effects, the following may be needed for some productions: crepe hair, liquid body make-up, latex (for skin blemish effects, etc), false fingernails, nose putty, stage blood, etc. You will need packs of hair bands, clips and pins, not to mention combs and the like. And there must always be on hand a plentiful supply of water, towels, tissues and soap.

False beards and moustaches

Just sticking on a false beard or moustache will not do. Inevitably they always look false to the audience, especially if there is a very young face behind.

The beard or moustache must be conceived and applied in coordination with the general facial make-up. It is far more effective and cheaper to use crepe hair which can be bought in braids. This must first be soaked in water and teased out. Then, when it is dry, it can be separated into broad strands and cut into pieces which should be much larger than the intended beard or moustache. Both beards and moustaches should be built up piece by piece on the face, then fixed with spirit gum, thus building up layers that make it seem more like natural hair growth. The appearance at first will be of a long, ragged growth, but once it has dried the whole thing can be trimmed with scissors to whatever shape is desirable and looks natural for the actor's face. A spirit gum removing agent will be needed to remove the hair at the end of the performance.

Props

There are props and props: those which the smooth running of the play depends on, and those that are merely the whims of individual actors and directors.

In the first group are those explicitly required by the stage instructions of the play, or implicit in the text: the letter which conveys essential facts, the gun found by the body in the library, the bottle of champagne cracked open in the final scene, etc. There are also those implied by the setting of a particular scene: crockery and cutlery if the scene is set around a dining table; books and newspapers if it takes place in a library. All these can be further differentiated into those which are pre-set and those which have to be brought onto the stage by an actor at some point, or added by a stagehand if there is a time change.

There are also personal props for which the actors themselves must be made responsible. Someone else may have to provide them, but it is the duty of the actor to make sure that they are in the right place at the right time, and to keep them safe in the meantime. These are such items as walking sticks, cigarette lighters or cases, briefcases, etc.

Some personal props may be specified in the text or stage instructions, but many may be the result of the interpretation by the actor of the character being played. The presence or absence of all props must ultimately be decided upon by the director, who may also have his or her own whims: deciding, for example, to place vases of flowers around the set to suggest springtime, or that there should be a lot of empty bottles on the table in a bar scene, to suggest that the characters have been drinking for a long time. The director may also decide on the bare minimum of props, using only the absolute essentials.

The props supervisor (also known as the props 'master' or 'mistress') is ultimately responsible for all props being present during technical and dress rehearsals and during the run of the play, and for ensuring that they are in the right place at the right time. They do not, however, have to run around gathering every single prop themselves before this stage, though they will doubtless need to undertake some frantic, last-minute searches. Organisation is everything. They will need to draw up a checklist of all the props needed, distribute copies to all cast and crew, and go around checking who can supply what, or who knows someone who can. There will need to be sections on such a checklist for descriptions of the items, names, phone numbers and email addresses for the suppliers, addresses (to arrange collection of any large items), and a section for notes on any other important details (e.g. 'valuable, not to be left in theatre overnight', or 'wrong period but looks similar', etc).

The props supervisor will also have to make many other checklists of various kinds in the course of one production: what is being kept where; what is to be pre-set (and where precisely); which actors are providing their own personal props (and which personal props come from other sources); what items are to go on the props table; any items which must be provided fresh for each performance (e.g. food and drink), etc.

Over the course of the whole production the following sequence of tasks needs to be observed, with many being undertaken concurrently:

- Read the play carefully, making notes of all the props you think will be necessary *before* you meet with the director to discuss the matter. When you do meet with the director make sure that there is an agreed storage space for the items you will be collecting, which you can have access to at all times prior to the technical rehearsal. If all else fails, you may have to make space in your own home.

- Make a new list incorporating the director's requirements. Leave spaces for later additions. Provide sections for descriptions of objects, names of providers, phone numbers, email addresses, postal addresses, any special requirements, and other important details.

- Remember: there are likely to be changes during the rehearsals, with both director and actors making it necessary to add or remove certain props. Check regularly with all involved, and attend rehearsals occasionally (especially those in which whole acts are run through) to see if there have been any changes that no one bothered to tell you about.

- Initial checklist. It is a good idea to attend an early complete run-through of the play. If this is not scheduled, it may be necessary to attend several rehearsals, to ensure that you can talk to each member of the cast. Go through your list with everyone, noting the names and details of anyone who can provide the items required. Some people may prove elusive, so you should obtain a list of everyone's phone numbers as soon as possible, and, if necessary, check them out over the phone. Don't forget to ask the crew and the director too: they may also have just the items you are looking for.

- Some props may simply not be available, especially if they are old-fashioned and specific to their period. It may therefore be necessary to make mock-ups, e.g. of a period baby's cot, of a crystal radio set, etc. You will need to find out who is a dab hand at knocking up such items, and make sure they can be made in time for the technical rehearsal.

- For a play with a historical setting it may be necessary to do a tour of all the local antique and second-hand furniture and charity shops. If things precisely in period cannot be found, you will need to have researched the period sufficiently well to know what can pass muster at a distance on the stage: you cannot be expected to obtain a real Ming dynasty vase, for example! You also cannot be expected to actually *buy* such items, of course, unless they are going at such a bargain price that it is worth the outlay. It will be necessary to clear with the director beforehand just how much money you can spend on props altogether. Many shop-owners will willingly lend you items for the duration of the production, on condition that they are well looked after (kept every night in your own home if necessary). They may require you to sign a receipt. Also they can often be tempted by promises of free advertising in programmes and, with some hard bargainers, you might even agree to cite them as sponsors on your posters and handouts (though this will need to be cleared with your society's committee).

- Don't just rely on people's descriptions of the required articles. Go and see them for yourself, or, if it is practical, ask the actor or crew-member to bring the item to a rehearsal for you to examine it. It may be too big, too small, the wrong colour, or the wrong shape.

- If it is a complex production with a large number of props, don't try to do everything alone. If you need an assistant or two, tell the director and try to find some reliable people. You may need help not only during the collecting stages but also during the performances, if a large number of items have to be moved around in a short time. Think ahead and plan for this.

- Make up your specific checklists:
'What is where?'
'Pre-set'
'Personal'
'Props table'
'Fresh each night'
... and possibly some others specific to a particular production.

- If there are many and complex props which are truly essential to the smooth unfolding of the action, it would be wise to arrange with the director that some of the final complete run-throughs of the play before the technical rehearsal be done with such crucial props on hand.

- In the final days before the technical rehearsal you should be running frantically around making sure that absolutely all the props are ready and available. All props should by now have been collected and kept in store. Never rely on anyone to bring anything 'on the night'.

- Before, during and after the technical and dress rehearsals, and indeed all the performances of the play, you must check and re-check that all props are there, none are missing, that they are in the right place, and that nothing is broken and needs to be replaced. At the end of every performance make sure that everything is stored safely away for the next one. Things left lying around are liable to disappear. You must check if the stage is securely closed off when it is not in use during the daytime before the next performance. If it is not, many of the pre-set items may have to be stored away to avoid theft.

• After the last performance, of course, you must ensure that everything is returned to its rightful owner. It may be inconvenient to do this on the last night itself, especially as most people will, hopefully, be in a celebratory mood. If people can stow things away in bags and boots of cars, all well and good, but otherwise it may be necessary for you to take them home yourself for the night. If the owners of your venue allow you to leave things overnight after the last night, then it will obviously be best to leave it all till the morning after. Valuable items borrowed from shops and the like would be best stored away in the usual place, or in your own home for the time being, until you can return them at suitable times with effusive expressions of gratitude. Items bought for the occasion or specially constructed should be retained for possible future use.

Props table

The props table is a table, as large as space and access will allow, set up in the backstage area, as close to the stage as possible, and in some circumstances actually on the stage but behind the back cloth, cyclorama or wing flats. The table must not be so large, however, that it impedes access to the stage for actors and stagehands. For most productions one table will suffice, and in fact one table prevents confusion in the actors' minds: it is better if he/she knows that there is only one place where that crucial prop should be. For complex productions it may be necessary to have at least two tables, however, one each side of the stage, just as long as everybody – the props supervisor and his/her assistants, and the actors – knows which prop must be set on which table and which table they must be returned to after use. This becomes absolutely crucial, for example, when one actor has to take an item offstage, which will then be brought on by another actor at a later stage in the performance.

The props on the props table are those which must either be taken onto the stage by actors at specific points in the production or set during a scene change by the props supervisor. They can be very small items, such as jewellery or a letter, or larger items, such as a tray with tea-pot, or a pile of old documents. All props should be laid out neatly on the table and not just dumped in a pile. It must be possible to see quickly exactly where something is. If an item is no longer needed for the rest of the play it can be placed in a box or other container nearby. If necessary, and to avoid confusion, labels can be used – affixed *to the table* and not the items (you don't want an actor wandering onto the stage with a label dangling from his prop!) – to identify items clearly. This will be crucial if there are two similar items, e.g. 'Mr Brown's letter' and 'Mrs White's letter, with ring inside'. It will be necessary to check the layout of this table thoroughly before the technical and dress rehearsals and every other performance of the play. The props supervisor will need to be on hand near this table every night during the run, to make sure that everything is in the right place at the right time. If he/she cannot be present for one performance, there must be a stand-in available who has attended both the technical and dress rehearsals and is familiar with everything that needs to be done. Simply telling someone what to do and leaving it at that is a recipe for disaster.

Prompter

To prompt or not to prompt? There are arguments for and against. Certainly to have a prompter during the rehearsal stages can be readily justified. But during the performances?

At the stage during rehearsals when actors are putting down their books for the first time, it can be very helpful indeed to have someone on hand following the scene with the script in hand. Actors master their lines at different rates and have different psychological needs: some will pause and, after a while, the words will come to them; others will go completely blank and be utterly helpless until someone tells them the next word; and there are yet others who will push on, blithely paraphrasing. There is also the problem of knowing when to stop the actor who uses a wrong word or expression and when to let them go on till the end of their speech.

A good prompter must get to know all the actors, their preferences and needs. They must be considerate and patient nurses, caring as much for the wilful child as the helpless one. A few simple questions suffice: 'When do you want me to prompt you?', 'How long shall I wait?', etc. As a rule of thumb it is best to agree on a general principle with all the actors, making exceptions only when requested. It avoids disagreement and annoyance, for example, if the principle is agreed upon that the prompter will say nothing unless the actor says the word 'Prompt'. It is best, therefore, to have the same person as prompter throughout. It is not a good idea just to use whoever happens to be on hand or not acting in that scene, although in an emergency, if the normal prompter is absent, it is better to use another actor, who knows what is needed, than a friend of a friend who has just happened by that evening. A regular prompter can and must keep notes of all changes to the text and cuts that are made, and mark them in their own copy.

At the stage when the actors are coping without their books for the first time, it is especially important not to interrupt them to point out errors. It is far better to make notes and then go and have a chat with them at the end of the scene. Actors will appreciate this help enormously. They will probably have been aware of many of the errors themselves, but just could not find the right word at the time, so reminders have to be discreet and considerate.

No actor is ever completely sure of all their lines and will make errors even at advanced stages of rehearsals, so it may be advisable to have a prompter on hand in subsequent rehearsals, even when things are flowing smoothly, just following the text and making notes. If persistent offenders are discovered (the actor who always gets certain phrases wrong, but seems unaware of the fact, for example), it would be wise to inform the director and let him or her handle the actor discreetly.

The presence of a prompter at the technical rehearsal can be very useful, especially as it will be necessary to cut large chunks of the play on that occasion to concentrate on technical matters. This is liable to result in many of the actors becoming confused about where they are supposed to be and what they are supposed to be doing. As lines become closely associated with moves and location in the mind of the actor, the words are likely to be forgotten easily in such circumstances. However, the prompter may also become confused by the unexpected chopping and changing necessary in a technical rehearsal. Prompting can also be provided by the stage manager on this occasion, who will be very much in control of matters and can let the actors know what they should be saying when a specific technical cue is imminent. The SM will have a lot of other matters on their mind, however, and will not be able to pay much attention to the actors generally.

A big issue and an important question to settle well in advance is whether to have a prompter during the actual performances. In the drama group of which I was chairman for many years, we had a general principle of not using a prompter during performances. The principle was in place before I joined the group, and I found it to be a good one. The main reasons for not having one are psychological. Knowing that someone is there to prompt at all times can encourage laziness in learning the words properly. Nothing breaks the theatrical illusion as thoroughly as an actor suddenly calling for a prompt, or stepping aside to hear a prompt shouted out from the wings. Far better to muddle on, even if it means losing a few lines, or changing them in some way, while at all costs endeavouring to stay in character. Sooner or later, and usually sooner than one fears, the play will get back on track, with the right line coming to the actor who is having trouble or another actor providing a line which leads everyone back to the text. There is a golden principle that should never be forgotten: the audience do not notice mistakes unless you make them aware of them! With the exceptions of famous speeches in well-known plays, the text will be generally unfamiliar to most of the audience; they will not know what the actors are supposed to be saying. Therefore, carrying on and speaking with conviction will lead the audience to assume that it is all a legitimate part of the play. Of course, one does not want this kind of situation to arise too often, or the whole play will become incoherent. But it is undoubtedly the best and most convincing way to deal with occasional mental lapses. It happens to all actors at some time or other and one should always be prepared for it.

Should the unlikely situation arise in which an actor dries completely and the whole performance freezes, it should not be forgotten that the stage manager is just in the wings, following the book at all times. To avoid disaster, he/she can shout out the line if necessary. Some insecure amateur actors argue that they are indeed amateur and should not be expected to learn their lines like professionals. This is the time to remind them that this is a negative perception of the amateur: you can have a professional attitude without being paid for what you do. A professional actor has the same kind of mental abilities and memory skills as any other human being. He/she may have had to learn lines more often than other mortals, but there is no special skill or technique which has had to be mastered.

There are, of course, exceptional circumstances when one can justify having a prompter during performances: when an actor has had to be replaced at short notice and someone else has had to learn the part in a short time; when there are one or two actors who are notorious for forgetting their lines, but there was no one else available to play the parts; when the play is for only one or two actors, and little help can be expected from other actors onstage; and other circumstances, when the demands on the actors are in some way unusual (as in some plays by August Strindberg and Samuel Beckett, for example).

Musical director

It is only possible to give very general advice about the role of a musical director in the production of a play. Musical performance involves artistic skills of a different order to acting and these are well outside the scope of the present book. But this very fact needs to be remembered when incorporating live musical performance into a play, especially if the musical components are extensive, as in Brecht plays or musical comedies. While the musical items need to be included in the normal rehearsals of the play on some occasions, this amalgamation cannot take place until the musical rehearsals have reached a fairly well-accomplished stage. This need not be until full run-throughs of the play a week or so before the technical rehearsal. The reasons for this are obvious: to rehearse one musical number may take an hour or more. Rehearsing several pieces will take up your whole evening's rehearsal time. But you cannot just leave musical rehearsals until the last week. If the play involves many actors in singing songs at various points, it is best to run a separate schedule of song rehearsals alongside the acting rehearsals. These need only be for one or two individuals at a time, together with the musical director. I did this very successfully with a production of Brecht's *Schweyk in the Second World War*, which involves the main characters in numerous songs integral to the meaning of the play (see Figure 6).

However, the musical director needs to feel that he/she is very much a part of the whole production, and should be encouraged to attend actors' rehearsals, to get a feel for the play. The musical director may also come up with useful suggestions about how the songs are to be interpreted and staged, and he/she will need to understand the director's overall vision for the production. For the Brecht production I was very lucky to have the participation of a very skilled musical director, Gordon Willis, who is also an accomplished performer, composer and adapter, and who involved himself in every aspect of the production.

Finding a good musical director is, of course, a major challenge, and no play involving live musical numbers should even be contemplated before confirming at the very start that a reliable musical director is available. Director and musical director need to be chosen at the same time. If there is no one in your group who has the necessary skills, the most likely place to find such a person would be in local schools and colleges, and also in churches. Many music teachers are involved also in local musical activities: running a school orchestra, taking part in private musical evenings, and very likely running choirs in local churches too. There is bound to be someone in every community who would leap at the chance to become involved in a play with live music and singing.

Of course, if the singing is demanding, not just a matter of some rowdy drinking songs in bar scenes but performances of intricate melodies, the musical director will have to work closely with the director in the casting of the play, to ensure that actors who may be ideal for certain characters also have the requisite vocal range for the songs they will have to perform.

Date	University Players lunch-times	re- Schweyk? Early evening (5 - 7 pm.)	Song rehearsals Evening after 7pm.	Other times
Mon.10/10		(with Gordon) Philip: 6.15.	(with Gordon) George (and Bill?): 7.00pm.	
Tues.11/10	(with Peter) Iris, Heather: 1.30pm.	(with Gordon) John: 6.30pm.	(with Gordon) Hazel: 7.30pm. (at rehearsal by 8.15pm at latest)	
Weds. 12/10		(with Gordon) George and Bill: 6.00pm.		
Thurs.13/10	(with Peter) Iris, Heather: 1.30pm.	(with Peter) JHHN Howard: 6.00pm. John : 6.30pm.		
Fri. 14/10	(with Peter) Howard: 1.15pm.	(with Gordon) Bill: 5.45pm. Philip: 6.15-7.00pm.		
Sat. 15/10				Hazel with Gordon at 3.30? (Please check with each other whether OK)
Sun. 16/10				Run-through at 2.30.pm. Could Gordon OR Peter play piano?)
Mon. 17/10	(with Peter) Iris, Heather: 1.30pm	(with Gordon) George and Philip: 6.00-7.00pm.	(with Gordon) Howard: 87.00pm. Hazel: 7.30pm.	
Tues. 18/10	(with Peter) John:1.30-2.00.	(with Gordon) George and Bill: 6.00-6.40pm. Howard:6.40-7.00pm.		
Weds. 19/10		(with Gordon) George and Bill: 6.00-6.30pm. Heather: 6.30pm.		
Thurs.20/10	(with Peter) Iris, Heather: 1.30pm.	(with Peter) John: 6.00pm.		
Fri. 21/10		(with GQrdon) Iris, Heather: 6.00-6.30pm. George and Philip: 6.30pm - 7.30pm (N.B. Rehearsal of sc. 8 at 7.30.pm. Could a pianist be present please?		
Mon. 24/10		(with Gordon) George: 6.00pm. Iris: 6.30pm.	(with Gordon) Howard: 7.00- 7.30pm.	N.B. at 7.30pm in music Dept ALL SINGERS and ALL MUSICIANS for run-through of ALL SONGS and ALL MUSIC!
Tues. 25/10		(with Gordon) Iris, Heather:6-6.30. Philip: 6.30-7.00pm.	(with Gordon) John:7.00- 7.30pm.	N.B.(with Peter) Howard:6-6.30.

Figure 6. Music and song rehearsals.

Choreographer

Many of the points to be made about the role of the choreographer are similar to those already made about the musical director. Advice given can only be general, the skills involved are of a different order to acting, and the choreographed sequences need to be rehearsed separately before they can be incorporated into the play. However, choreography involves not only dance – which is likely also to involve music and therefore also the musical director, unless it is recorded – but also such activities as man-to-man fighting, fencing, processions, demonstrations, etc. It is often not necessary to have a choreographer if the director is experienced and trained in some of the basic skills needed for staging such kinds of group interaction. I have had no choreographic training but have learned how to stage fights, mass movements and demonstrations and the like. I would, however, need to bring in an expert in fencing were I to attempt to stage the final scenes of *Hamlet*. Plays involving scenes of country dancing, ballroom dancing, etc, clearly require some expertise in those fields, but you will not necessarily need the services of a fully fledged choreographer to rehearse them. One individual for whom it is a passionate hobby will probably provide all the help you need. As with the search for a suitable musical director, a specialist in drama and movement who is willing to help out can often be found in a local school or college.

Stagehands

Not everyone who just happens to be around will do as a stagehand. It is best to gather, well in advance of when they will be needed, a group of strong, sturdy helpers who can devote themselves solely to the task of being good stagehands, which means basically moving the various bits of the set around and making sure they are in the right place at the right time. One needs firm promises and commitment from people you know you can trust to be there when needed. With a small drama group it may be necessary for members of the cast and crew to help out too, when this does not conflict with their other commitments in the production. Husbands, sons, brothers and boyfriends, wives, daughters, sisters and girlfriends can often be persuaded to help out, and fellow workers or fellow students may also be open to persuasion. Exactly who is needed to do what and when must naturally be planned carefully beforehand. This planning and organisation is essentially the job of the stage manager, always consulting, of course, with the director, set designer and set builders.

The work is predominantly physical. It involves heaving a lot of things around: rostra, flats, pieces of furniture, etc. Stagehands may also be required before the technical rehearsal to clamber up ladders to adjust the angles of lights. In fact, they should be brought in at the latest by the last run-throughs prior to the technical rehearsal, and ideally welcomed along at a much earlier stage. Like everybody else in a production, stagehands need to feel that they are essential to its success, and that everyone appreciates their contribution. To gain such appreciation they also need to do their part and show interest in the play: reading it, familiarising themselves with the moves of actors, becoming aware of how long scenes are, when major scene changes take place, how much time can be allowed for such changes without causing the play to drag, etc. It is a good idea for the stage manager, together with all the stagehands, to attend a full run-through of the play some time before the technical rehearsal, so that they can all discuss together what needs to be done, and how to distribute the tasks. They will probably be needed to help with the construction of the set as well, although the extent to which this will be necessary will vary from production to production. Basically they will have to do whatever the stage manager requires of them, and it is difficult to be more precise than this, due to the fact that every show has different needs. They will also have to check in with the stage manager well before curtain-up every night of the run, so that he/she can be certain every task is covered. Should it prove impossible for one stagehand to be present on all nights of the run, so that his or her tasks have to be covered by someone else on those nights, this must be agreed well in advance and the substitute well briefed at the technical rehearsal, walking through the moves if necessary. Absolutely nothing must be left to impromptu decisions on the night, for this can well lead to errors and delays, affecting the whole performance.

After the last night, the stagehands are also a crucial part of the get-out, ensuring that every piece of the set is dismantled carefully and safely, and every large item removed from the stage, to be stored or returned to its owner. As menial as the tasks may seem, the stage and whole backstage area will then need to be swept, cleaned and cleared of rubbish, if the drama group is to make a good impression on the owners of the venue and hopes to produce a play there again.

DESIGNING AND BUILDING A SET

In the absence of a set designer, the director, stage manager, and any practically minded individuals in the group can get together to come up with a workable set. Generally it is advisable for the director to provide some indication of his general design concept and any specific aspects he wishes to have incorporated. Rehearsals cannot really begin until set design has been determined, so this has to be fixed very early in proceedings.

If one of the group is designing the set it is useful to adopt certain standard conventions indicating the various parts of it. This makes it easier for the set builder, who may well be a different person, and his team to construct the set exactly as required (for the standard conventions and symbols used in set design see Figure 7).

Some of these conventions are used in the simple design for a living room set shown in Figure 8.

Even at the early stage of selecting the play, the director must have some clear ideas about how it is to be staged. Once rehearsals have been started no major changes should be undertaken in the design of the set, or this will confuse everybody involved and set everything back. The director will have to re-plot moves and actors will have to rethink many aspects of their performances. The planning of the lighting also depends on a fixed configuration of the set.

What kind of set is used for a production also depends, of course, on the nature of the stage, whether it has a proscenium arch, is in the round, has a studio layout, or is in an amphitheatre (see Figure 9).

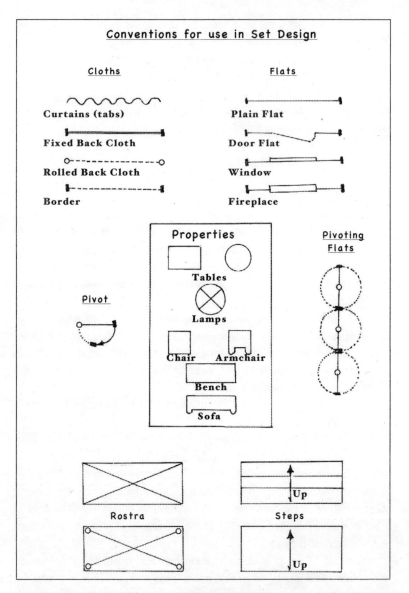

Figure 7.

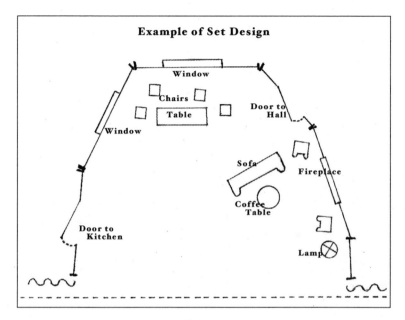

Figure 8.

If the director is skilled to some degree in the matter of basic set design, he will be able to come up with some sketches, however amateur the artwork, which others can transform into workable plans, and three-dimensional drawings. It is also very useful, once the plans have been agreed, for someone to construct a three-dimensional model of the whole set. This serves many uses: it gives actors an immediate sense of how their acting space will look; it gives some idea of relative spaces and sizes; it is a useful aid for the director in pointing out exactly where they want things to be, how lit, etc. The stage manager will also find it extremely useful in explaining to the stagehands their various tasks.

It may be possible to call on the services of free skilled help in both set design and construction. Students in local arts colleges and indeed their teachers, and even art teachers in primary and secondary schools, can often be tempted to participate. Students are often particularly keen to

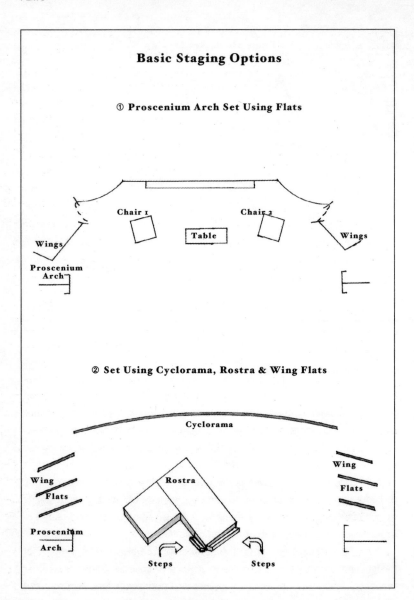

Basic Staging Options

① Proscenium Arch Set Using Flats

Chair 1

Chair 2

Table

Wings

Wings

Proscenium Arch

② Set Using Cyclorama, Rostra & Wing Flats

Cyclorama

Wing

Flats

Wing

Flats

Rostra

Proscenium Arch

Steps

Steps

Figure 9.

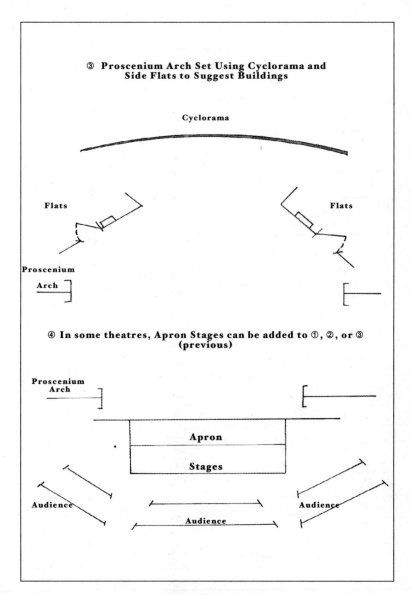

③ Proscenium Arch Set Using Cyclorama and Side Flats to Suggest Buildings

Cyclorama

Flats

Flats

Proscenium
Arch

④ In some theatres, Apron Stages can be added to ①, ②, or ③ (previous)

Proscenium
Arch

Apron

Stages

Audience

Audience

Audience

Figure 9. (cont.)

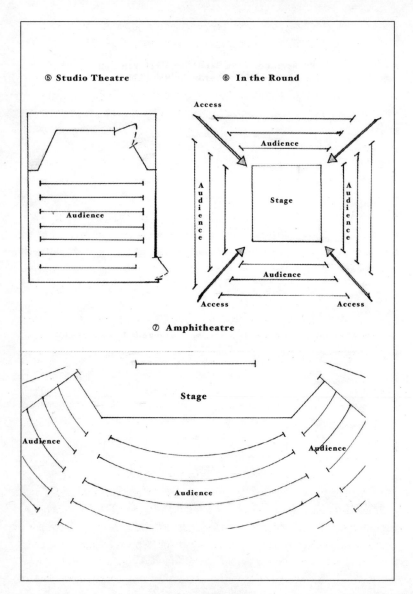

Figure 9. (cont.)

have a chance to use their skills and imagination in ways unrestricted by their syllabus. And teachers may even consider incorporating the activity as project work in their courses. There may also be retired designers of various kinds living in the area who would leap at the chance to do something creative in the public eye again. For our group in the south of England we were lucky to find a retired theatrical designer who could produce stunning effects with the minimum of means and expense. He was also aware of all the safety precautions that had to be taken in building a set.

Safety precautions are an aspect of a production which many amateur groups are unaware of and need to inform themselves about: all flats have to be firmly fixed, bolted down if necessary; rostra have to be held firmly in place, as do steps; there must be no rough wooden edges or sharp metal corners, etc, which can cause serious injuries; and any angled supports or beams must be clearly marked with luminous tape if in dark areas backstage, as must the edges of any steps giving access onto the stage. In fact it is not a bad idea to appoint someone as safety officer to keep a check on all these aspects of the production.

Needless to say, especially because of the safety concerns, it is crucial to obtain the help of a good carpenter and experienced odd job man. The construction cannot be left in the hands of well-meaning DIY addicts of little real competence beyond following manufacturers' instructions. The same applies to the electrics: if there are lights and other electrical equipment to be installed on the set, a qualified electrician must be used, with all cables being safely taped down so that no one can trip over or become entangled in them.

Whatever technical resources a group may have access to, basic or extensive, it is possible to create an effective set through imaginative use of the means available. Complex does not necessarily equate to good, and a simple set can make a powerful contribution to the whole production. A basic three-wall set with a few doors and windows behind a proscenium arch is easy enough to construct. Its effect will depend on how the set is dressed, in terms of furnishings, drapes and the like, and how it is lit. More abstract sets to serve multiple scene changes can be constructed with an assortment of rostra and steps (see Figures 10 and 11).

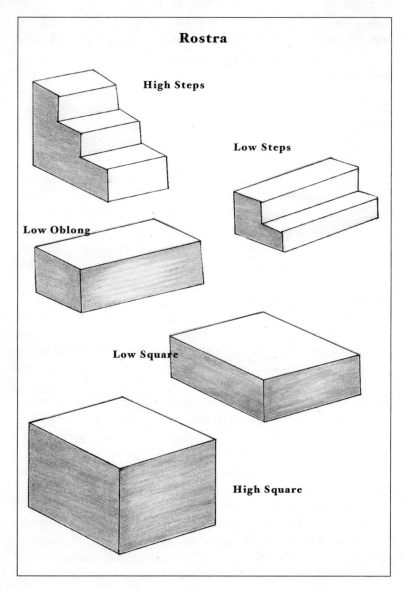

Figure 10.

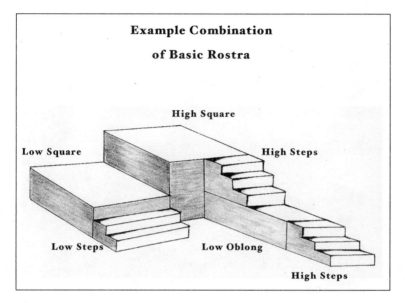

Example Combination of Basic Rostra

Figure 11.

Rostra usually come in a few basic shapes and sizes, like building blocks, with matching steps. A set of them can easily be constructed by a skilled carpenter. They require strong wooden frames, with a firm wooden floor on the topside, and can be covered with hard-wearing, floor-covering material, which can be painted according to need.

They can be assembled in various imaginative ways. A few possibilities are shown in Figure 12.

A set of scaled-down models of the rostra available can be made for the director to play around with on a table, until he/she comes up with a combination that will work for the play. Shakespeare plays can be staged very effectively on such simple sets, consisting of various levels, with evocative lighting of a plain cyclorama behind.

Finally, one rather obvious point needs to be laboured: designers and constructors of sets need to be constantly aware of the costs of their undertaking. Spending on tools, wood, paint, fabrics and other materials

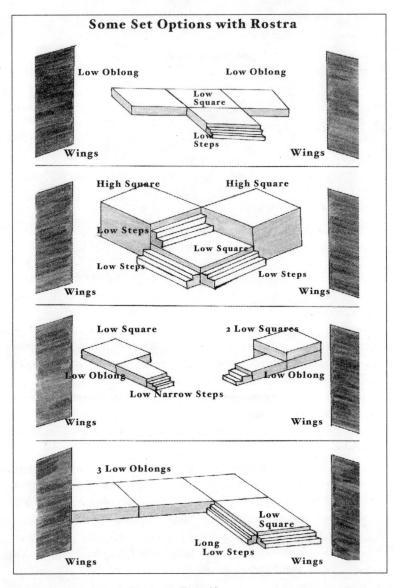

Some Set Options with Rostra

Figure 12.

can soon mount up, and each item of expenditure should be checked with whoever is controlling the budget for the production.

USING ACTORS' GAMES AND EXERCISES

During training courses for actors many kinds of games and exercises are practised, to develop flexibility of the body as well as responsive mental attitudes. Many actors carry over these practices into their subsequent professional careers. Some such games and activities are undoubtedly very useful and effective. It is doubtful, however, that many amateur groups will have the time and patience to indulge in many of them, unless their relevance and usefulness is immediately obvious: pretending to be animals is obviously useful preparation for a show in which some actors will be playing animals; physical interaction and fighting are useful for plays with war scenes; inducing unusual states of mind is helpful if actors are playing emotionally disturbed characters, etc. With only a few hours available in an evening for any given rehearsal, however, the director must choose very carefully if he/she wishes to include such activities. If the intention is merely to enable the actors to relax and trust each other, this is likely to be easier to establish in an amateur group by means of various social events away from the rehearsal space. Not all professional actors are in any case convinced of the usefulness of regular games and the like before rehearsals. The respected actress Eileen Atkins has said in an interview: 'Those games do one thing, they make sure that everyone talks to every- body, that everybody knows each other's name, and that you all know that you're a group, and you should be pretty relaxed with each other by the time you act. But for my money, that should be a given before you start, that you always talk to everybody! The same things would have been done getting there a quarter of an hour before rehearsal, and all having coffee together.'[1]

Some useful books explaining the principles of drama games and including many imaginative activities to try out are included in the 'Resources' section at the end of this book.

PUBLICITY

The old adage that all publicity is good publicity only applies to play productions if it is favourable. No one wants bad reviews. But reviews generally appear far too late to affect the ticket sales of amateur productions, anyway, unless your group is able to stage long runs. With the average run being no longer than four or five days, a review of the first night which appears later in the second day of the run is only likely to affect sales for the last few days. And not everyone reads local newspapers that thoroughly. Preview pieces, on the other hand, can be very useful.

It is really best to have someone whose sole job is organising publicity, though, as with many other responsibilities in a small group, it may be necessary to double up on this. As the major part of the publicity campaign must be accomplished well before the technical rehearsal, it would be practical for someone handling make-up or doing some prompting to double up as publicity organiser. Other people working backstage and the stagehands themselves can also take on this job.

Whoever takes on the responsibility cannot start soon enough in exploring the possibilities for publicity within a reasonable radius of the performance venue.

Radius of advertising

How widely you advertise depends on several factors. In a built-up area with good transport connections you can spread your net more widely. Your bottom line should be the answer to the question: how far could someone be expected to travel on a weekday evening to see an amateur production? Subtract or add a few miles for seasonal factors: will the play be performed on balmy summer evenings or cold, wet winter nights? Time must also be allowed for getting to the venue after the working day and getting back home within a reasonable time afterwards. These are considerations for all productions, but there will also be considerations specific to your venue which need to be explored. Brainstorming with fellow members of the group will yield many ideas about the most suitable methods of advertising, the likely markets and the best locations for posters and handouts, etc.

- What age groups will the production appeal to? How can they best be informed about it?
- What local bus and train routes run near your venue? People on these routes, without cars, are more likely to be tempted. But if they have to make too many changes they are likely to be put off. Is it possible to put up posters at the relevant stations and near the relevant bus-stops?
- Are there facilities for food and drink nearby (pubs and restaurants)? People are likely to be attracted to your performance if they can make an evening of it, especially on Friday and Saturday nights, with a drink and food before or after the performance. Try to have the local pubs and restaurants (and takeaways) display your publicity prominently.
- Does your play have the potential to attract audiences with special interests? One such interest might be in particular periods of history, and if the play is set during, for example, the Second World War, it would be worth advertising in local retirement homes, military establishments, museums and historical societies. Or perhaps it deals with specific social problems of interest to minority groups, such as racial conflict, unmarried mothers, gays and lesbians, immigrants and so on. If it includes singing and dancing, it would be a good idea to advertise at local institutes and schools teaching these skills.
- What free magazine advertising is available in the area? Many local cultural magazines and 'What's On?' style publications offer free listings for events or charge very reasonable rates for advertising. Samples of the magazines available in your area can be obtained at libraries, arts centres and information centres, including tourist information offices, if your district attracts such visitors.
- Local TV and radio stations often feature reports on cultural activities and provide free announcements during certain programmes. It is worth watching or listening to the relevant programmes to discover what sort of format the announcements have and thus what information would be required. A few phone calls to the studios should also clarify things.

- The local press should be scoured for similar coverage as that provided on TV and radio. As well as accepting paid advertisements, the local newspapers will also often have free listings on certain days, usually near the end of the week. It is therefore important to make sure that one gets coverage the week *before* the first night. They might also be interested in having a preview article, either by a member of your group or by one of their own journalists. In this case some photographs are usually welcome. But be sure to have a few really impressive images with which to supply them. One photograph of people in makeshift costumes with ill-fitting wigs and moustaches on an unfinished set will be more likely to deter audiences than attract them. Over many years I built up a good relationship with one local journalist, on whom I could always rely to provide us with good preview coverage if I notified him in time.

- Posters. Where can you put them? Shops, supermarkets, libraries, cultural centres, information bureaux, church halls, bookshops, in fact virtually everywhere within your catchment area prepared to take them. It will require the participation of every single member of the drama group: posters don't stick themselves up! A good idea is to give a set number of posters to each member of the group, with more if they can guarantee to use them, with advice on the best places to have them displayed, or you can give the able-bodied ones distinct areas which they should cover. Some tips need to be given on how to ensure that the posters are indeed displayed where one wants them. It is not sufficient just to go into a shop, for example, ask if they will display a poster and then leave one with the person behind the counter. One needs to be a little assertive and make quite sure before leaving the premises that the poster is up where promised, even if this causes some slight annoyance. It can all be handled in an amicable fashion, however. I once spent several afternoons with a friend and a car-load of posters going round several suburbs of a large city, trying all manner of shops and other establishments. The most effective manner I found was jovial politeness. If an assistant is vague and uncertain, politely ask to talk to the manager. Offer to put the poster up yourself, if they will show you where it would be convenient. If the location seems to be a poor one, suggest where you would ideally like to put it. Have a bag of various kinds of sticking materials, such as transparent tape, glue sticks, pins, etc. Some managers may be willing, but fussy about how it is done. Do not be satisfied with a vague promise by an assistant, as they push your poster under the counter, to put it up somewhere later. It will more than likely be neglected. Have some handbills with you too. These can be left in small piles in locations such as public libraries.

- Mailing. Usually a mailing list takes some time to set up, and is unlikely to be a suitable way to advertise for a newly established group. Naturally any members who are not directly involved in the current production will have to be mailed with details, and perhaps some copies of posters and handbills. To establish a mailing list for interested members of your audience, a section on contact details can be included in the programme for the performance. Nowadays email addresses as well as postal addresses should be provided where possible. Just mailing organisations and other places where one wants to advertise is not advisable, for the same reasons that leaving a poster with a busy shop assistant is unlikely to be effective: your publicity is likely to end up in someone's litter bin.

- Staging events. If your play involves some exciting visual aspects – a pantomime, for example, with several actors dressed as animals – or uses colourful period costumes, it is a good idea to arrange for some kind of public event to attract attention. Having first gained permission from the relevant authorities, a group of actors could wander around *in costume* in local shopping malls, shopping centres, markets, or other central locations, handing out handbills and even carrying posters on placards. And musical accompaniment would be sure to attract attention. Needless to say, such events are best arranged for very shortly before the first night or during the run. If they are arranged too early, people will have forgotten about your show and thrown your handbill away.

Making posters and handbills

There are so many ways of making professional-looking posters and handbills nowadays: one just has to explore what services are available locally and survey members of your group for skills in design, and computer graphics especially. Posters can be made entirely through computer programs and printed out at least in master copies, which can then be duplicated or photocopied in colour at local print shops. Someone will have to go round comparing prices, to get the best bargain. Usually the more you do, the cheaper it is. It is difficult to give much general advice in this area, and it is good to allow your designers some freedom of expression, but generally a poster should not be too complex as this may obscure the basic information you wish to get across. A few simple, bold images will suffice for the main design, and be sure to stress the selling points of your production. If it is by a famous playwright, display his or her name prominently. If it is a hilarious comedy, let people know this. Was it a West End success recently? Remind them. Above all, make sure all the essential information is displayed clearly and accessibly. Essential means information regarding how to purchase tickets and find the venue. Accessible means that a passer-by can find such information easily on the poster, without having to bend down or crane their neck sideways.

This is the basic information that needs to go on every poster:

- The name of your group.
- The title of the play.
- The name of the author.
- Names of musical composers (if relevant).
- Dates and times of the performances.
- Name of performance venue and location details. A sketch-map may be useful.
- Box office. Location, opening times and phone number. If the tickets will also be sold in other local outlets, such as shops, etc, then details must also be provided.
- Contact phone number for the group, for general enquiries.

PROGRAMMES

Programmes are a luxury you can, at a pinch, do without. They are, however, an attractive aspect of productions and serve many useful purposes. Apart from simply providing information about who is playing which role, the names of the technical crew, and the scene divisions within the play, they can serve to provide acknowledgements of all those who have in some way contributed to the success of the production. Background on the historical context of the play can also be provided and they also give the director a chance to write something about his or her concept for the production, justifying, if necessary, why it is being staged in such a way. A brief biography of the author can also be of interest. When the group has become established and some of your performers have become known to regular members of your audience, you can consider including brief biographical notes on them, but in general it is wise not to encourage a false sense of stardom among amateur actors. Community spirit and equality are more valuable qualities to encourage. An important element should be a section about the drama group in general: what your aims are, what you have accomplished and your plans for the future, with an invitation to other interested parties to join you, in whatever capacity. Contact details for your membership secretary and information about a website, if you have one, should also be included.

In their design and production, programmes share many aspects with posters and handbills. Indeed it is a good idea for them to share the same design features, so that there is consistency of design throughout the production. This should also extend to incorporating elements of the production itself in the design of posters and programmes. For a production which I had set in the period of the Thirty Years War (1618–1648), not only were the costumes in period but also images based on the work of a contemporary artist were used in both poster and programme design.

Depending on your budget, programmes can vary from the very cheaply produced to the more expensive, glossy kind. Prices should reflect not only your costs in producing them but also what they offer in terms of content. You can probably afford to distribute a very cheaply produced programme completely free of charge. In the early days of the Southampton University Players we produced quite satisfactory four-page photocopied programmes by copying the material on both sides of an A4 page and then folding it along the middle (see Figure 13).

ooooooOoooooo

SOUTHAMPTON UNIVERSITY
PLAYERS

present

SCHWEYK

IN THE SECOND WORLD WAR
by BERTOLT BRECHT

An amusing and bitterly ironical play about the Nazi occupation
of Czechoslovakia with songs and music by HANNS EISLER

Directed by DAVID CARTER

November 3rd, 4th, and 5th at 7·45pm

NUFFIELD STUDIO THEATRE

ooooooOoooooo

Figure 13. Cover of simple four-page programme.

BERTOLT BRECHT [BIOGRAPHICAL NOTES]

1898 - 1956. German Dramatist, poet, director and theoretician. Began his career as a dramatist with a series of experimental plays heavily influenced by Expressionist techniques. The first play in which his Marxist preoccupations came to the fore was *The Three-penny Opera* (1928). For this, as for his opera *The Rise and Fall of the City of Mahagonny* (1930), the music was composed by Kurt Weill. In 1933, with the advent of Hitler, Brecht left Germany, going first to Scandinavia and then to the U.S.A. Between 1937 and 1945 he wrote some of his best and most well-known plays: *The Life of Galileo* (1937-9), *Mother Courage* (1938-9), *The Good Person of Setzuan* (1938-41), *Schweyk in the Second World War* (1942-3) and *The Caucasian Chalk Circle* (1943-5).

Southampton University Players wish to acknowledge their gratitude to all those who have lent properties for the production or have contributed in various other ways to its success, and especially to the Department of Music at the University.

SOUTHAMPTON UNIVERSITY PLAYERS: FUTURE EVENTS

December 5th and 6th, Nuffield Theatre Studio	— An Anthology of Verse, Music and Narration organised by John Birtwhistle, the University Fellow in Creative Writing.
in the week of February 20th, Nuffield Theatre	— *Major Barbara*, by Bernard Shaw, directed by Adrian Vinson.

If you are interested in joining Southampton University Players and perhaps taking part in the above events, then please come to the auditions on Monday 14th November [for John Birtwhistle's Anthology] and on Friday 18th November [for Major Barbara]. Both auditions take place at 7.30 p.m. in the Common Room of the Department of Physics.
Further information can also be obtained by telephoning The University [559122] and asking for ext. 609 [Trevor Gilson] or ext. 326 [Leslie Johnson].

oooooo0oooooo

Figure 13 (cont.). Back page of simple four-page programme.

As your group becomes more successful and, hopefully, begins to make a little money, you can progress to glossy, colourful, multi-page programmes incorporating photographs and, if you can persuade them, advertisements by local businesses, as well as any sponsors or other organisations which have contributed in some way.

Remember to explore the opportunities provided for attractive poster and programme design on dedicated websites and in desk-top publishing programs. It is possible nowadays to produce very professional-looking programmes with the aid of up-to-date computer technology.

DIRECTING A PLAY

Directing, along with the art of acting, is probably the most difficult aspect of play production to explain and advise on. Directing and acting are, by their nature, highly individualised. There are as many directing styles as there are directors. Consequently I can only explain the ways in which I prefer to do things when directing, with hints occasionally of what others might prefer to do.

The audience perspective

In general terms, the director is an ideal member of the audience, having a concept of the whole and seeing how it all fits together. He/she is able, however, to do what a member of the audience never can: intervene and suggest how things might be developed and changed. Always in the mind's eye of the director should be the play as the audience will be seeing it. This is not to say that the whole production is somehow pre-formed in the director's mind; it is constantly developing and undergoing change. But that audience perspective should always be there.

It is especially important for the director to be constantly on the look-out for whether any actors are masking other actors from some members of the audience, and even standing too far back or to the side, so that they cannot be seen by most of the audience when they speak. The range of the audience's sight lines in the theatre must be constantly checked during

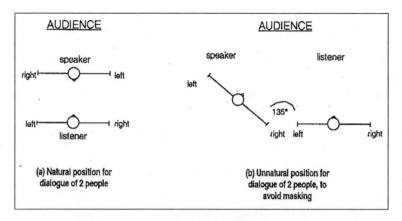

Figure 14. Angled dialogue.

rehearsals (see the discussion on sight lines in the section of 'Planning a Rehearsal' entitled 'Blocking').

An actor must be alerted if he/she is masking another actor when the latter is speaking. In normal conversation we tend to face each other directly; but on the stage it is often necessary to stand at what may seem to be an unnatural angle of about 135 degrees away from each other. In other words, one must stand half towards the audience while turning one's head towards the other actor. It is a convention which, if handled subtly, the audience is hardly aware of (see Figure 14).

The actor's perspective

The ideal director will have seen many performances of all kinds of plays, have read and studied many and done quite a bit of acting. Personally I have found the latter qualification to be one of the most important. Even if a director cannot act particularly well, some experience of, and sympathy for, the problems and challenges facing actors will prove indispensable. Some directors who have not acted themselves can sometimes have unreasonable expectations of what actors can achieve. Knowing how you would like to be handled as an actor undoubtedly helps in the guiding of others.

Guiding and heeding

It is indeed a guiding process. There is not, nor should there be, a master-plan, like a blueprint, from which the edifice of the play can be constructed. The director should have some idea in advance of how events in the play will be interpreted, and, one hopes, a coherent view of the whole. But these are all starting points rather than predetermined goals.

The director must be prepared to modify, adapt, and change at every stage of the process, following his or her own changing perceptions, and also heeding the ideas and suggestions put forward by the actors, designers, and indeed everyone else on the team.

In casting, the director looks for germs of possibility within the actor. The actor's contribution is then to develop this germ into a fully convincing organism.

The set

There are some practical considerations which the director needs to take into account from the start. Some of these will be difficult to change later, for artistic reasons and also because of time and budgetary constraints. A few of these have been mentioned already: it is necessary early on to decide on casting, technical crew and, perhaps most importantly, the overall concept of the production and its general look, in order for the precise nature of the set to be agreed with the designers and construction crew.

Cutting the text

A controversial issue with many actors, and indeed audiences, is how and to what extent a director decides to cut a text. It happens much more than most audiences realise, and is usually only noticed with classics when famous lines or sequences are cut in some way. Shakespeare's plays are almost always subjected to cutting of some kind. Sometimes the cuts are unintentional, as when actors forget whole sequences, but carry on with conviction, so that it is difficult to tell whether the cut was intentional or not. Often, however, these, and other classic works, are cut for reasons of length: they would otherwise make for an extremely long evening in the theatre. There are also sequences of which the meaning has become obscure with the passage of time, or in which a long list of classical allusions is incorporated that would simply be boring for modern audiences. Little is lost by omitting them and much gained in clarity of plot development and perspective. In more modern plays cuts are often made for the convenience of a particular production. A joke or an allusion might be made, which has long lost its topicality and will almost certainly fall completely flat with the audience. Unless its omission will leave some illogicality in the text, it is best to cut it. Nowadays matters of political correctness are often at issue: is it best just to omit a certain phrase rather than deal with the embarrassment or offence it might cause? It is the director's responsibility to make the decisions about such matters, and they should be made early, if possible before the start of rehearsals, so as not to confuse the actors. It may only be discovered during the course of rehearsals, however, that a particular sequence does not work for some reason, and in that case a decision about cutting it should be made as soon as possible. In such a situation, an actor may wish to protest against a director's decision, especially if they feel they have a way of making the sequence meaningful. An actor may also feel that the sequence is crucial to his or her concept of their character. If it is a minor character the actor may also resent losing a large chunk of their role. When such conflicts of interest arise, the director must resolve the matter as diplomatically as possible, giving the actor the benefit of the doubt if he/she argues strongly. The matter can always be reconsidered at a later stage.

Blocking

Once all this has been worked out the director needs to consider how he/she wants the actors to move about the set in each scene. This is known technically as blocking. Directors will vary greatly in how they do this and to what extent they do it at all. Small scenes with a few actors often do not need very precise planning beforehand, but scenes involving crowds and large groups, or just numerous small groups, need careful organisation. These plans and directions need not be set in stone. A director's handling of blocking is as likely as any other aspect of their style to reflect their personal psychology: do they like everything ordered and under control, or are they happiest when they can constantly change and modify? But some kind of planning in advance is always needed, and sketching out the basic movements for every scene provides a framework for everyone to work within. It is the scaffolding which enables the edifice to materialise. As rehearsals proceed, modifications will be made and even major changes will sometimes be needed, but this rough draft, this outline, is vital at the beginning. (Further practical advice is provided on blocking in the chapter on rehearsals.)

Conducting rehearsals

What the director actually does during rehearsals is again hard to prescribe specifically. He/she must be wary of jumping in too quickly and frequently with comments and suggestions as the actors are stumbling their way through the text on the first few occasions; and even later, when it seems that the actors are getting the hang of their roles, interventions should only be made when things are perceived to be going wrong, or when a particularly inspired thought will be likely to help an actor. It is best to run through small chunks, discuss and make suggestions, and then run through them again until everybody is reasonably content, with the director, as ever, seeking to bring out ever more subtle and convincing performances from the actors.

At all times, too, the director must have an eye on those little technical weaknesses that actors are prone to succumb to from time to time: speaking upstage in a way which audiences will not hear, masking other actors, upstaging (forcing another actor to turn their back on the audience), forgetting the audience's sight lines, failing to project their voices sufficiently strongly, etc. These are not such crucial omissions in the early stages of rehearsal, but need to be dealt with firmly as the technical rehearsal approaches. Also, if allowed to persist too long the actor is likely to indulge in them unconsciously and find it difficult to eradicate the habit at a later stage. A director's assistant or other willing member of the crew can help a lot in agreeing to watch out for such things on the director's behalf.

Overall responsibility

The director must also be aware that, whatever problems arise at any time, the buck finally stops with them. If some member of the crew fails to do their job, if certain tasks are not carried out (costume not ordered, music not ready, props missing, someone ill), the director must, by hook or by crook, ensure that the omission is rectified, the person replaced... or must simply go and do it themselves.

2. REHEARSALS

LEARNING LINES (ADVICE TO THE ACTOR)

Actors should not be daunted by the task of having to learn lines. There are as many different ways of doing it as there are actors. Some have developed very idiosyncratic ways of mastering them. The clearest and most useful advice I have come across is to be found in the book *Being an Actor* by Simon Callow:

> It is, in my experience, impossible to learn *words*: you learn the thought patterns of the character, of which the words are the inevitable expression. If you learn the *words*, you lay down rail tracks which you must follow, and any sense of the thoughts and impulses which gave rise to the words is very hard won. The only way for me to learn, at any rate, having nothing remotely resembling a photographic memory, is to ask of each fresh line, how did this line give rise to that? And try to reconstruct the mental journey. Hence, very logical characters are very easy to learn, those with eccentric thought-patterns, like Lord Are in Bond's *Restoration*, extremely hard.[2]

There are geniuses among the famous professionals who can come to the first read-through with all their lines learnt. No one expects this as a matter of course, not even in the professional theatre, let alone on the amateur stage. It is only the most accomplished professionals who can do this and still maintain the flexibility necessary to adapt and modify their performance during the course of rehearsals. Many lesser mortals find it difficult to introduce changes into the way they have memorised the text. One should not worry about this matter of learning the lines too much. Provided one works away at it regularly, associating the words always with what one is actually doing on the set, and bearing the nature of the set constantly in mind, the words will eventually spring to mind automatically in association with the actions performed. It is people who try to learn lines in the abstract who have the most difficulty remembering them.

You should not, in any case, expect to learn your lines before you have started to understand the character you are playing. You may, of course, never understand the character completely, but you will progress towards more perfect understanding as rehearsals progress. You also need, first of all, to move towards an understanding of the play in general and the function of your character within it. Learn to move around the set and feel what is the right behaviour for your character, and also how you interact with the other characters, and start to develop some three-dimensional awareness of each scene you are in. Then will be the time to really attempt to master the lines. By this stage they will have started to stick because they are associated with the whole context in which they are to be uttered.

It is, however, true that final mastery of the character and your performance of it cannot come until you can speak the lines with a fair degree of fluency, with only the odd error and forgetfulness here and there. Mastery of the lines enables a kind of take-off in your performance. You can now begin to play around and experiment with the character more confidently.

A director may set all the cast a deadline by which the lines should be learned. This is useful in the same way as the prospect of death is said to sharpen a man's mind. Deadlines are one of the most effective creative tools devised by mankind. You may or may not have mastered the lines on time, but one needs that deadline to focus the learning process.

In practical terms, learning lines means hard slog, day in, day out, at home, on the bus, on the tube, in bed, out of bed, and over a pint of beer. Some actors have been known to put their lines – or some of the longer speeches, at any rate – on bits of paper and stick them up around the house, so that they can go over them any time at a moment's notice.

Thinking of the rhythm and getting into it, as well as thinking very carefully about the meaning, undoubtedly aids the process. Thinking through each speech also enables you to bring each word alive and convince the audience that, though you both know better, your words have been coined in the moment you utter them.

A great aid in the learning process is to have a willing friend sit with you occasionally and read all the other characters' parts while you speak yours. I have personally found it useful to record the sections of the play where my character appears, reading all the other parts myself and allowing short gaps where my character should speak. You can then practise your lines with a finger on the pause button, stopping it when your cue comes. At the end of your speech, release the pause and listen for the next cue.

Finally, the lines will only become firmly fixed in your memory when you have practised the scene a sufficient number of times in at least a simulation of the set with all the other actors acting with you. The lines in the end come to acquire a logic of their own: you say something because it is the only thing for your character to say in that particular situation, performing those particular actions, together with that particular person. The memory of your lines seems to be somehow imprinted on the situation in which you are acting. This is why an actor tends to forget a whole part, save perhaps a few memorable lines, very soon after the performance is over: he/she is no longer moving in the world where those words were meaningful. It is almost as if the words uttered are part of a hologram, which appears completely real for as long as it endures. When the hologram vanishes, however, the words themselves no longer have any medium in which to exist.

READ-THROUGH AND PREPARATORY STUDY

Whether it is felt that a read-through of the play with all the cast is a necessary pre-requisite will depend on the director's preferences, as well as whether the actors themselves feel it would be useful, and on whether one was incorporated into the auditioning process. It has the benefit of helping everyone get a feel for the relationships of the characters to each other in an informal way. It is probably wise therefore to read it through without any introduction or interruptions by the director: just let the actors go about it in their own individual ways. Let them play around with it. The director may even gain a few useful insights in the process.

Whether there should be much preparatory study and discussion of the play will again depend on the director, as well as on the complexity and difficulty of the piece. Certainly everyone involved needs to have some idea of the director's general aims and intentions for the production, his or her concept for the style of the set and costumes, etc. Generally, however, most actors prefer to get on as soon as possible with the business of rehearsing and to discover what the play is about by doing it. Too much critical analysis and theory about meaning only hinders the process of acting.

The actors themselves may well have to do some homework, exploring the historical background of the play, understanding the manners and attitudes to morality in a specific period, and generally researching unfamiliar aspects of their character: for example, their character may be a Catholic while they are not, or they have to play an unmarried mother, a war veteran, or whatever. They may feel it necessary to discuss some of these aspects of their character with the director, to see how they all fit together with the main themes of the play. If one comes across a puzzling scene during rehearsals, it is always possible to stop the scene, sit down and talk about it before proceeding.

One should not expect the meaning and significance of every line to become clear at the same rate. Some parts of the text may remain obscure for some time, and it may take a long time before it occurs to the actor how best to deliver the words. When in doubt, and if the problem of how to deliver a line persists, it is generally best just to keep on doing it, rehearsing it, not thinking about it too much, and eventually, with luck, it will somehow, by intuition, come right. There was one actress in a play I was acting in who wanted to discuss every one of her lines with the director. The director finally lost patience, because the woman was constantly holding up the whole rehearsal, and said to her, 'Look, if you have any questions come and talk to me after the rehearsal. Just get on and do the scene'. Meaning and significance tend to creep up on you slowly; only rarely do they strike you in one fell swoop.

PLANNING A REHEARSAL SCHEDULE

The rehearsal schedule for an amateur production must of necessity be different to that for a professional group. Professional actors can be expected to be present as and when required, unless they have other contractual commitments. For amateur rehearsals it is necessary to take into account the intricate web of different jobs and lifestyles amongst the cast. Most participants have jobs and families which for them must sometimes take priority over their hobby of amateur drama. Once the thankless task of planning a rehearsal schedule has been completed, however, and everybody's needs met as nearly as possible, the director has the right to expect that actors and crew will make some personal sacrifices to maintain it.

For the sake of continuing good relationships, the director must do his or her best to please as many people as possible. And it will have to be the director who draws up the rehearsal schedule, as this involves making decisions about some basic priorities, and dividing the play into rehearsable chunks. Once the director has drawn up the basic guidelines, a director's assistant can be very useful in contacting all the actors (the crew can be considered separately), and gathering the basic information required. It will have to be the director, however, who finally decides what to rehearse, when and with whom.

How long a rehearsal period do you need?

This decision also depends on a variety of factors. How often in any given week can rehearsals be arranged? For how many hours on each occasion? Are there any music, dance or movement sequences which will need extra rehearsal time? At what times can the actors be available? How long is the play?

As a general safety precaution it is wise to allow for more weeks of rehearsal than you think you will need. This will allow you sufficient time to deal with setbacks. Having established a schedule, however, you should stick to it as closely as possible. The fixed deadlines work in the unconscious minds of the actors in their own mysterious ways, encouraging them to prepare for tasks in a timely way. Add a few extra rehearsals here and there by all means if it becomes necessary, but never subtract. It may also become necessary occasionally to modify the actual content of a rehearsal if you discover that some scenes are proving to be more demanding than originally thought; but if you drop one scene at the expense of another, be sure to pay special attention to the dropped scene next time round. It is also a good idea to programme in a few blank rehearsals, which can be filled at a later stage, when it becomes clear that some sequences need more detailed work, or if an actor has been absent through illness, etc. Generally, however, the principle of sticking to the schedule should be followed as strictly as possible. Chopping and changing will only generate insecurity, which can jeopardise the quality of the whole production.

Assuming that most of the actors are working full-time, and that they can only manage perhaps two evenings a week, with the occasional Saturday afternoon – with the stipulation, of course, that they will have to be present *every night of the week before the technical rehearsal, at the technical and dress rehearsals themselves, and every night during the run* – one should allow at least six weeks from the first rehearsal until the technical rehearsal. For the production of a play by, say Alan Ayckbourn or Terence Rattigan, with an average-sized cast (usually eight to ten) and two or three acts, which can be broken down easily into rehearsable units, this should be quite sufficient. For a play with songs and music and many complicated scene changes, it might be necessary to extend this period by several weeks. More than two evenings a week would also be advisable for demanding plays, though one should try to arrange things so that individual actors will rarely be required for more than two evenings a week on average. It might also be necessary to arrange for longer rehearsals at weekends, using perhaps an occasional Saturday or Sunday afternoon if all are willing.

It is also wise to limit each rehearsal in terms of hours, except when it is necessary to run through a whole act or the whole play. Pushing the actors too hard will be counter-productive. On a weekday evening some actors will not necessarily have many reserves of energy, so it is wise to let actors go home just as soon as you have run through their scenes. Always try and see your schedule from the actor's perspective. Thus one might start at seven or half past, which allows everyone to get home from work and grab a bite to eat, or at least snatch a sandwich on the way directly to the rehearsal; then, with a short break about halfway through (no more than five or ten minutes), aim to finish before nine, or nine thirty at the latest. Try to organise things so that people who need to get away asap have their scenes rehearsed first, though this may not always be practical. There is then plenty of time for those who wish it to pop down to the pub for an hour. These periods of social drinking can be useful for bonding the cast together and mulling over broader aspects of the production. They are a luxury extra, however, and getting adequate rehearsal time must be the main priority. For run-throughs of whole acts it may well be necessary to go on until ten, and for a run-through of the whole play till ten thirty or so. Run-throughs are therefore best scheduled for weekend afternoons.

Newcomers to the world of amateur drama should be made aware that it is not going to be a casual affair, attending rehearsals just when one feels like it. They are making a commitment, and should feel a responsibility to everyone else involved. If one person does not turn up for a rehearsal, there is only a limited amount of work that can be done on his or her scenes. Having to talk to an empty space, or someone drafted in as a last-minute replacement, sets back the development of the performance every time it happens.

Rehearsing music, songs and dances

If there are musical, song or dance sequences in the play, special rehearsals will have to be arranged for these; when and where they take place will depend very much on the availability of the musical director and/or chore-ographer, and also on when the actors/singers can be available. For basic mastery of the pieces short sessions should be enough, a half hour or so at the most, but these must take place on a regular basis, running parallel to the normal play rehearsals. You will obviously need to find a location with at least a piano. For music and songs, probably a small space will suffice, though a larger area may well be necessary for dances. As a rough guide-line, each piece should be rehearsed at least twice a week, concurrently with the normal play rehearsals, and then, at some point to be decided by the director, incorporated into run-throughs of individual acts and then of the whole play. It is best for the musical performances to be at a fairly advanced stage before this occurs, as it will be disruptive of the rehearsal as a whole if the musical director or choreographer needs to interrupt continually in order to ask for a sequence to be done again. More advice than this cannot be usefully given, as much has to be left up to the judgement and expertise of the musical director or choreographer. Needless to say, final decisions about how much rehearsal time to allocate to music, song and dance must be left to the director and, to avoid misunderstandings and confrontations, the musical director and/or choreographer should be made aware of this from the start. I have already included a sample rehearsal schedule for songs and music for my production of Brecht's *Schweyk in the Second World War* (see Figure 6). This was designed to dovetail with the normal rehearsal schedule for the actors (see Figure 15).

Checking availability

The director (or assistant) needs to check the availability of all the actors (and musicians and singers, if relevant) before the rehearsal schedule can be drawn up. A simple questionnaire should suffice. To save time and effort these can be handed out and completed at the auditions or read-through of the play. There will need to be columns for names and contact details (be sure to include daytime contact numbers, mobile phones and email addresses), sections to indicate which days they can be available on a regular basis, and which times are preferable for them, e.g. from 6pm, from 6.30pm, from 7pm, etc, and until what time, e.g. till 8pm, till 8.30pm, till 9pm, etc. For weekends, blocks of time can be specified e.g. Saturday and/or Sunday morning, afternoon or evening, with any time limits. There should also be a section for listing any specific dates on which they are not available, and a section for any other special considerations, such as 'possible late arrival on Tuesdays', 'needs to get away as early as possible on Mondays', 'needs a lift home on Wednesdays', etc. (A sample questionnaire is available at www.kamerabooks.com/downloads.)

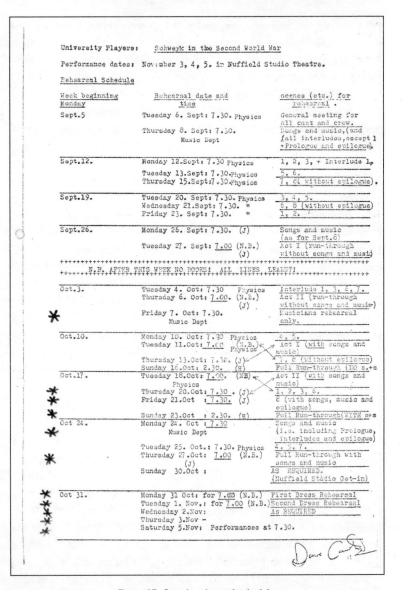

University Players: Schweyk in the Second World War

Performance dates: November 3, 4, 5. in Nuffield Studio Theatre.

Rehearsal Schedule

Week beginning Monday	Rehearsal date and time	scenes (etc.) for rehearsal.
Sept.5	Tuesday 6. Sept: 7.30. Physics	General meeting for all cast and crew.
	Thursday 8. Sept: 7.30. Music Dept	Songs and music,(and all interludes,except 1 +Prologue and epilogue).
Sept.12.	Monday 12.Sept: 7.30 Physics	1, 2, 3, + Interlude 1.
	Tuesday 13.Sept: 7.30.Physics	5, 6.
	Thursday 15.Sept:7.30.Physics	7, 8(without epilogue).
Sept.19.	Tuesday 20. Sept: 7.30. Physics	3, 4, 5.
	Wednesday 21.Sept: 7.30. "	6, 8 (without epilogue)
	Friday 23. Sept: 7.30. "	1, 2.
Sept.26.	Monday 26. Sept: 7.30. (J)	Songs and music (as for Sept.8)
	Tuesday 27. Sept: 7.00 (N.B.) (J)	Act I (run-through without songs and music)

+++
++++++ N.B. AFTER THIS WEEK NO BOOKS! ALL LINES LEARNT! +++++++++++++++++

Oct.3.	Tuesday 4. Oct: 7.30 Physics	Interlude 1, 3, 6, 7.
	Thursday 6. Oct: 7.00. (N.B.) (J)	Act II (run-through without songs and music)
✱	Friday 7. Oct: 7.30. Music Dept	Musicians rehearse only.
Oct.10.	Monday 10. Oct: 7.30 Physics	4, 5.
	Tuesday 11.Oct: 7.00 (N.B.) Physics	Act I (with songs and music)
	Thursday 13.Oct: 7.30. (J)	7, 8 (without epilogue)
	Sunday 16.Oct: 2.30. (H)	Full Run-through (NO s.+m)
Oct.17.	Tuesday 18.Oct: 7.00. (NB) Physics	Act II (with songs and music)
✱✱	Thursday 20.Oct: 7.30 . (J)	1, 2, 3, 6.
✱	Friday 21.Oct : 7.30. (J)	8 (with songs, music and epilogue)
✱	Sunday 23.Oct : 2.30. (H)	Full Run-through(WITH s+m
Oct 24.	Monday 24. Oct : 7.30 Music Dept	Songs and music (i.e. including Prologue, interludes and epilogue)
	Tuesday 25. Oct.: 7.30. Physics	4, 5, 7.
✱	Thursday 27.Oct: 7.00 (N.B.) (J)	Full Run-through with songs and music
	Sunday 30.Oct :	AS REQUIRED. (Nuffield Studio Get-in)
✱ Oct 31.	Monday 31 Oct: for 7.00 (N.B.)	First Dress Rehearsal
✱✱✱✱	Tuesday 1. Nov.: for 7.00 (N.B.)	Second Dress Rehearsal
	Wednesday 2.Nov:	As REQUIRED
	Thursday 3.Nov -	
	Saturday 5.Nov: Performances at 7.30.	

Figure 15. Sample rehearsal schedule.

Rehearsable units

For rehearsal purposes most plays must be broken down into manageable units. Many present unwieldy masses of text with characters appearing and disappearing according to exigencies of the plot. Sometimes an actor may only have a few lines to speak at the very end of a scene; or they may appear in it only briefly elsewhere. In such cases one can afford to be generous and allow an actor to be absent from some rehearsals of such scenes.

There is no set rehearsal pattern to fit all plays, and a director must tailor the schedule to suit the piece. In some plays there may be whole scenes which lend themselves very conveniently to rehearsal as units, but in others a scene may have to be broken into sections. For example, the first part of the scene could be between two characters, the middle part between four, and the final part between the first two again. The first and last parts can therefore be conveniently rehearsed together with only the two actors involved needing to be present. It is clear, therefore, that the director must read and re-read the play, breaking it down into units which can be rehearsed with the same groups of actors. There will, of course, come times when whole scenes will have to be rehearsed in their entirety, and all the actors will just have to wait their turns. But in the earlier stages of rehearsal one can afford to be more flexible.

To make things clearer, here is a breakdown of the first act of a hypothetical play:

A, B, C and D are the characters (or the actors playing them) in the play.

Act I.   1. A, B and C talk together for three pages. Then A exits.
          2. After A's exit, B and C continue to talk together.
          3. A returns and A, B and C continue to talk. A and B exit.
          4. After the exits of A and B, C is alone for a while. Then D enters and C and D talk for a while.
          5. A and B return, and A, B, C and D talk together. D exits, and A, B and C continue to talk. A and B exit.

6. After the exits of A and B, C is now alone. Soon D enters and they talk briefly before D exits again.

7. After D's exit, C is alone. C goes to the phone, dials a number, and speaks to someone on the phone. B enters, unseen by C, and overhears the phone conversation. C puts the phone down and sees B. C and B argue. C exits angrily leaving B alone.

(End of Act)

It should be quite clear that certain combinations of these artificially created units, or chunks, of the play can be rehearsed together, with only those actors involved present.

Thus A, B and C can rehearse units 1 and 3 together; B and C can rehearse units 2 and 7 together; C and D can rehearse 4 and 6; A, B, C and D can only rehearse unit 5 together. In the early rehearsals and especially for the blocking, therefore, an evening's rehearsal of the first act could be scheduled as follows, to use the time most economically, to prevent too many people from having to wait around for too long, and to let as many people as possible leave as early as possible:

7.00pm	B and C (for units 2 and 7)
7.30pm	A, B, C (for units 1 and 3)
8.00pm	Break
8.05pm	A, B, C and D (for unit 5)
8.35pm	C and D (for units 4 and 6)
9.00pm	Rehearsal finishes

It can be seen from this breakdown that it will be possible to let A arrive by 7.30pm and leave by 8.35pm; B can also leave by 8.35pm; and D need not arrive until 8.05pm. Poor old C, obviously the hero/heroine of the drama, has to stay all evening, but there may well be other parts of the play where he/she can be let off more lightly. Obviously the schedule should have some flexibility, and the actors should try to arrive ten minutes ahead of time if possible, in case things have been going faster than expected.

Also, scenes will occasionally take longer to rehearse than expected, and actors may have to wait around a while before their turn. But one needs a framework to work with, and actors should not be unduly worried if a director is flexible with the timings. Notice that it is not always necessary to rehearse units in sequence, though this will become necessary later. Also, it will gradually become possible to rehearse larger units, so that units 1, 2 and 3 can be rehearsed together as one (involving A, B and C), and 4, 5 and 6 together (A, B, C and D). There will be times when actors will just have to wait around: they can always wander off into a corner and mumble their lines to themselves.

The schedule above has been drawn up from the ideal perspective of the director, but actors' lives may not allow them to be so obliging, and compromises may have to be made.

Number and frequency

How many times do you need to rehearse any given scene and how often? The simple answer is: until it works. But in fact you never finish rehearsing any scene: it is a continuous process of modification, development and polishing, even during performance. But there are a minimum number of rehearsals necessary, which a director gets a feel for over time, and each part of a play should be gone over at least as frequently as every other part, with the exception of a few scenes that may need more rehearsing than others for technical reasons (complex crowd scenes or ones with parallel sequences of dialogue overlapping, etc). Basically no part of the play should be left to look after itself because it seems superficially straightforward. Everything is important if a balanced, convincing performance is to be achieved.

It is advisable to rehearse every part (scene, unit) of a play at least once a week throughout the whole rehearsal period. If some sequences are clearly not up to scratch, additional rehearsals must be fitted in for them or they can be rehearsed in any periods on the schedule left deliberately blank for such purposes (mark such occasions 'as required' in the schedule). Also, on every evening when a sequence is being rehearsed, it should be run through *at least twice*, and possibly three times depending on time available. In the early stages of rehearsal, the first run-through of a sequence may involve many interruptions by the director, but then the actors need to be given the chance to run it through again. If necessary, a third run-through after comments and discussion may be helpful. Hence, in making the schedule, even short units of text should be given half an hour or so at least.

At regular intervals after the whole play has been blocked, run-throughs of complete acts should be scheduled (for a Saturday or Sunday afternoon, perhaps). This means that the actors can begin to get a feel for the whole, and it also helps them to gauge how the play should be paced. Such occasions are also good opportunities for the costume and props supervisors, and also the stage manager, to check out aspects of the play for which they are responsible. At least a couple of weeks before the technical rehearsal a run-through of the whole play is useful, to give an impression of how it is all developing. This will depend on the nature of the play and the length of the rehearsal period, although one complete run-through at least several days before the technical rehearsal is a minimum requirement.

It is also advisable to put boldly in black and white in the rehearsal schedule when the director wishes the actors to 'down books', i.e. have mastered their lines. In practical terms, with most amateur actors, this cannot be expected to occur earlier than one week before the first night. Set the deadline therefore at least TWO weeks beforehand – then, with a bit of luck, they might be near word-perfect by one week before! It must be added, however, that with plays for which the words are likely to present problems (Shakespeare, period drama in general, ones with a lot of songs, etc), the deadline should be as soon as is practical after the period of initial blocking and run-throughs of each scene. Finally, the director should not expect wonders. Be prepared to nag the actors frequently about their lines as the performances loom nearer, and leave the rest to conscience and the mysterious workings of the unconscious.

A sample rehearsal schedule has been included (see Figure 15) for my production of Brecht's *Schweyk in the Second World War*. It does not follow to the letter the advice I am giving in the present book, but no actual schedule ever would: one has to cut corners. The schedule has to be tailored to suit the requirements and circumstances of each individual production.

BLOCKING

Blocking is the common theatrical term for planning the basic moves and actions in a scene. It can be extremely simple or very complex, but need not be daunting to the inexperienced director. Some directors rely on it more than others, and in any case initial plans are often discarded in the course of rehearsals, or at least modified considerably. Complex scenes with a large number of characters obviously need some kind of planning if actors are not to collide, jostle each other around and create general confusion. With larger groups one must also, of course, pay careful attention to grouping for aesthetic effect. While one has to be careful in positioning actors on the stage in a play with only a few characters, the options are obviously fewer.

Masking and upstaging

In all cases, whatever the size of the cast, one of the functions of blocking is to ensure that the audience is focusing on significant parts of the action at crucial points. One actor must not mask another actor who is speaking, nor must they mask an actor whose facial reaction or gesture in response to another actor is crucial at that juncture. Good blocking alone does not suffice to avoid such errors, and the actors themselves must be constantly aware of where they are standing and what they are doing in relationship to the other actors. If they discover that they are masking someone else, they must move out of the way naturally, so that the audience is unaware of the purpose of the move. There are certain artificial conventions adopted in stage dialogues, which enable audiences to see the faces of both persons in a dialogue, without one actor masking the other (as shown already in Figure 14 in the section 'Directing a Play').

Upstaging is another error which can easily occur accidentally, but which some vain actors are often accused of indulging in to draw the audience's attention to themselves. It involves placing oneself upstage of another actor and causing him/her, whilst involved in a dialogue, to turn away from the audience. The effect is that the audience cannot see the face of the actor turning away and often cannot hear their voice either. Focus shifts immediately from the turning actor to the actor he/she is addressing. The effect can be used positively to great dramatic effect in the hands of a good director: if an actor enters centre backstage and all other actors downstage turn suddenly to look in their direction, they are immediately the centre of the audience's attention.

Sight lines

Another aspect of stage performance, which must be considered during blocking but is also important for each individual actor to be constantly aware of, is the audience's ability to see clearly everything that is happening on the stage: the sight lines. These have also to be considered, of course, in the process of designing the set, and will affect where items of scenery and pieces of furniture can be placed on the stage. It is very difficult for actors to retain awareness of the sight lines during rehearsals, especially if the rehearsals take place in a space dissimilar to the eventual performance space. It is advisable, therefore, to enable the actors to become acquainted with the stage before starting rehearsals. Let them walk around on it, see where the audience blind spots are. Is the auditorium a long rectangular box, or is it curved round with a curved seating area also, reaching beyond each side of the stage? Can those people who will be sitting on the far right or far left see everything that is happening on the stage? Should you avoid being in the upstage right and upstage left corners when you are uttering lines? Perhaps those sitting in the central area will be able to see your facial expression, but what of those sitting on the side aisles? They will have a completely different perspective. In some theatres there may also be a highly placed circle or balcony, meaning that you will need to raise your head at crucial points and not lurk too close to the cyclorama at the back of the stage (see Figure 16).

During blocking all these factors also have to be borne in mind. In fact, good blocking can avoid accidental ignoring of sight lines during performance. At the technical and dress rehearsals someone should be asked by the director to keep a check on the sight lines. Then, in giving notes and comments to actors after the rehearsal, the director can alert any offenders.

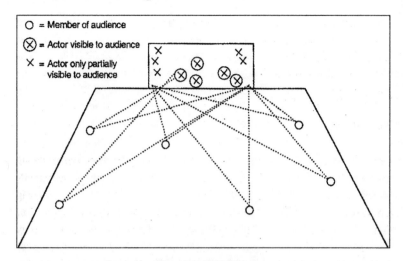

Figure 16. Sight lines.

Moves and positions

All that one needs to establish for most scenes fairly early on in rehearsals is where the characters move and where they stand or sit for most of the time, and how the configurations change when someone exits or another actor enters, or the situation changes in some other way. The finer detail and movements relating to the emotional state of the characters come with further rehearsal. As the actors grow in their understanding of the characters, the actor or director may suggest a change in the basic blocking arrangements (e.g. 'Maybe this whole scene would work better if she stood by the window rather than sat on the sofa', etc). But having the basic blocking in place provides a framework within which to start working on the text.

The director needs to work out a few such basic movements before rehearsing a scene, noting them down and also noting any changes that are made to his scheme at any time during rehearsals. The next time a scene is rehearsed, certain details will probably have been forgotten, at least by some of the people involved, and this can lead to little disagreements, such as when the actor protests, 'But last time we agreed that I would move here,' and the director retorts, 'No, I think I suggested you do it differently', etc. This is one of the tasks that a good director's assistant or production assistant can help with, keeping 'minutes', as it were, of the important changes and other decisions made. There is no need to note down every single move made by the actors, just those changes agreed on.

For complex scenes the director needs to draw up correspondingly detailed plans in advance. If it is found to be useful, the plan can be divided into nine squares to indicate the main stage areas (downstage right, downstage centre, centre stage left, upstage right, etc). It is useful to make many photocopies of the basic set plan, which can be used to make blocking plans on. For many scenes in Shakespeare plays this is really crucial. It really does not matter what symbols and conventions are used, as long as they are clear and unambiguous. Only the director really needs to understand them. One can make do with a simple variety of arrows and lines (in different colours and thicknesses, dotted or otherwise, as necessary), and numbers and letters, upper and lower case, together with a few scrawled notes. Arrows and lines can indicate directions in which characters move, letters can refer to characters, and numbers to other items as required. (See sample blank of a set and blocking plans for the first scene and part of the second scene of *Macbeth* in Figure 17. Initials refer to characters' names.)

Also useful when blocking scenes for the first time is the presence of a model of the set. Some movements may appear pointless to the actors until the director shows them on the model that, for example, they have to negotiate their way around a particular item of scenery.

THE FIRST REHEARSAL

By the 'first rehearsal' is implied the first rehearsal of each scene or rehearsable unit of the play. There will thus be many 'first rehearsals'. It refers to the very first time a scene is run through with the director in the rehearsal venue.

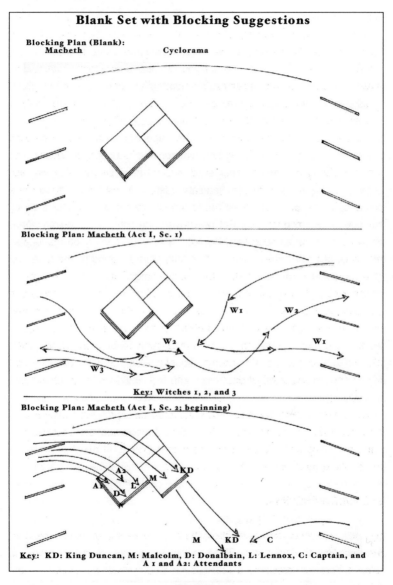

Blank Set with Blocking Suggestions

Blocking Plan (Blank):
Macbeth   Cyclorama

Blocking Plan: Macbeth (Act I, Sc. 1)

W1   W2

W2   W1

W3

Key: Witches 1, 2, and 3

Blocking Plan: Macbeth (Act I, Sc. 2; beginning)

A2   KD
A1   L   M
    D

M   KD   C

Key: KD: King Duncan, M: Malcolm, D: Donalbain, L: Lennox, C: Captain, and
A 1 and A2: Attendants

Figure 17.

The actor's tasks

Be prepared to be told what to do most of the time, where to move, stand and so on. This will be the case with all the 'first rehearsals'. Every scene of the play needs to be walked through, plotting the basic movements, with no concern for the way you read the lines or how you should develop your character, etc. You will be lucky if the director even allows you to say most of your lines. You may have your own ideas about how you should move in this scene and by all means let the director hear your suggestions, but it is best to avoid radical disagreements. You will have plenty of opportunity to try out your ideas in later rehearsals. Just help the director to get the scaffolding in place. And do not forget to note your moves in your copy of the play for future reference. Get used to adding and changing your notes whenever it becomes necessary. Do not rely on your memory of a particular rehearsal, because they will all become blurred in the mind by the time you have run through the whole play for the first time.

The director's tasks

Most of the advice given to actors for first rehearsals is also relevant to the director. In general the director should not attempt to achieve too much. You are familiarising the actors with the play and the imagined set, and checking if the action as you have conceived it will actually work in a real space with real human beings. Make sure that each scene is blocked in a very basic way and, if any actors ask detailed questions about their moves, interpretations of the text or development of their characters, politely postpone your decisions on such matters. If necessary for the actor's peace of mind, promise to have a chat with them about it after the rehearsal is over.

As a general rule it is a good idea to run through a scene one more time after blocking it, allowing the actors to speak all their lines and fit in the basic moves. This helps the whole process to cohere before going on to block another scene.

PROGRESS THROUGH REHEARSALS

Excluding consideration for the moment of the technical and dress rehearsals, progress through rehearsals after the first run-throughs and blocking is a fraught but rewarding affair. The course of a good production never did run smooth. Nor should one expect it to. But all the stress and annoyance has its rewards. Why else would anyone bother to do it at all?

Notes for the actor

Rehearsing is by turns fun and frustrating, rewarding and exasperating. You immerse yourself in a different world for a few hours and, if you are lucky, you find you have forgotten about your everyday cares and worries for the duration. There will be endless self-doubts and questionings, but one must persist. There is an unavoidable meeting with destiny ahead of you: the date and time is fixed. Willy-nilly, you will go on the stage on that day and perform. It is that awareness which drives you on, which focuses the mind and spirit, and which enables you to bring it all together. The sheer limit on time is a powerful creative force. From rehearsal to rehearsal you will just keep working away at your performance, learning the lines, developing your understanding of the role.

Working with a good director should be a mutually gratifying experience, but do not expect him/her to provide answers to all your questions and problems. The director can give you tips and make suggestions, but you must do most of the hard work yourself. It is also important to respect and aid your fellow actors. Be wary, however, of proffering too many suggestions to other actors: many may not welcome it. If you think you have a really good idea, and also if you are concerned about some aspect of a fellow actor's performance, mention it discreetly to the director. If the director takes your point, then he/she will raise it sensitively with the actor concerned.

You will also find that you can only make so much progress before you learn all your lines, but this should not be undertaken too early. Wait until the general shape of the play and your character are falling into place, you are familiar with the emotional rhythms of the play, and it is clear that the basic movements and relationships are established in your mind. Starting too early will probably fix your mode of expressing the lines too rigidly in your mind; starting when you feel it is the right time to explore the character more deeply will enable you to think through the logic of your character's language as you learn the words.

Do not expect that your performance will ever be perfect. There will always be aspects you want to work on and change. Even during the run of performances you will continue to discover new aspects to your character every night. One of the most accomplished amateur actors I know, John Souter, told me once, on the last night of a play I had directed, 'I feel I am only just beginning to understand my character. I could go on playing him for a long time,' He had, needless to say, been giving excellent performances every night.

Notes for the director

As can be seen from the advice to the actor, much of what the director has to do involves a kind of tentative support of the creative process: coaxing, encouraging, suggesting and enlightening. While having acquired, through much study and thinking about the play, insight into the way the whole coheres, you must also have the modesty to learn from the actors and from the experience of working with them on the text. Amongst other abilities, you must develop a quasi-musical sense of the pace, rhythm and interaction of the parts of the whole. No one else has such an overview of the whole production.

There will also be crucial and difficult decisions to be made at times: whether to cut some words and phrases, or indeed whole speeches, and whether an actor needs firmer handling or not. Directing is, after all, about people management amongst other things, and each actor will have their own little strengths and weaknesses and accomplish their tasks as actors in different ways and at different paces: some show a steady arc of development, others develop in fits and starts, and there are also those who do not appear to be making any progress at all but are in fact mulling things over in their own subconscious way, to come out suddenly with an almost fully fledged performance.

Decisions will also have to be made about whether to rehearse some scenes a little more than others. It will become obvious which scenes are somehow lagging behind, either in terms of expressive force or fluency, or just because the actors have not yet mastered the lines for those scenes. The basic rehearsal schedule should be respected but some additional rehearsals may be fitted in. Allowing for this in the original scheduling will make this process easier. There will also be occasions when you can sense that, despite the fact that the actors are making several technical errors, it is best to let them get on with it in their own way and run the scene through. One reason can be that they are clearly able to respond well and with suitable emotions to each other. Better then to sacrifice detail for the spirit of the thing. When doing run-throughs of complete acts or the whole play, it is also advisable to let the actors get on with it, let them run with it, allow the whole thing to live. Corrections and changes can be attended to in rehearsals of individual scenes afterwards.

When actors are beginning to put their books down there will need to be someone on hand to prompt (see the section on prompting). At first they may find it easiest to still carry their books in their hands, so that they can glance at them when necessary. Actors should tell you when they are ready to try to do it without book in hand, and you need to be patient with them. There is usually a temporary drop in confidence and fluency and therefore in the general strength of the performance for a while until the confidence is built up again. Actors tend to feel very insecure and vulnerable at this stage and need to be handled patiently and with special sensitivity.

ONGOING JOBS DURING THE REHEARSAL PERIOD

There are various tasks on which cast and crew need to work concurrently while the play is being rehearsed. Sometimes these tasks can be pursued independently, but often members of the crew and backstage helpers will need to attend the rehearsals to check out various facts and perceive how their own particular roles fit together in the whole production.

The set

In the light of any changes and problems in rehearsal, some alterations to the original design of the set may be necessary. Is there enough access space? Do the doors open the right way? Does that window need to be opened? Are there too many, or too few, steps? The actual building of the set needs to get underway just as soon as possible, though this will depend very much on available storage space, and how soon access to the stage can be gained. Small bits and pieces can be made and stored in someone's garage for the time being, and wood and other materials can be purchased or at least sources identified.

Props

Any additions, substitutions, changes? The person in charge will need to come to rehearsals occasionally to check the list with the actors and director. It will be an ongoing process right up to the technical rehearsal.

Costume

Measurements for costumes can be taken during breaks in rehearsals, or when an actor is waiting to rehearse. Costume-hire companies may need to be contacted and bookings made. For a modern-dress performance checks can be conducted with actors at rehearsals to see what items they can supply themselves. Fittings may need to be arranged.

Publicity

Posters and handouts should be passed on to the cast and crew for distribution at a suitable time.

Sound

Recorded music must be found and approved by the director, and possibly re-recorded in a suitable format for use during the performance. If there is to be live music, ongoing music rehearsals will need to be organised. Sound effects must be found or made and provided in a form in which they can be activated on cue.

Lighting

Should any amendments to the lighting arrangements be made in the wake of changes to actors' moves and/or modification of the set? Are any extra spots needed? More footlights? Any special lighting effects, such as strobe or lightning, etc? Any extra onstage lighting sources, such as the introduction of a table lamp on a desk, etc?

Stage management

The stage manager should be attending rehearsals regularly in order to make up the book, containing all cues and instructions, from which he/she will control the whole play in performance, and also to be on the look out for any difficult or impossible technical expectations.

Box office

The group's treasurer should be making sure that all arrangements for the sale of tickets are in order and that tickets are available for purchase as advertised.

THE GET-IN

The 'get-in' is the expression commonly used for the process of putting the set in place, decorating it, delivering all the props to the backstage area, fixing up the lights, testing the sound equipment and making sure that anything else technical is all ready, present and functioning before the technical rehearsal. In short it involves 'getting in' all the equipment you need.

Professional theatres may be able to allow themselves the luxury of several technical rehearsals and several dress rehearsals. With amateur groups you will be lucky to be allowed one of each, but one of each you *must* have. There is no way round it: every responsible production *must* have separate technical and dress rehearsals. And for both of these to run efficiently, a well-organised get-in is necessary. You just cannot have a good technical rehearsal if, for example, the set is only half made, if all the lights have not been positioned, angled and tested, or the sound equipment not tested, and if furniture and any other large props are not in place.

How long the get-in takes will depend on the nature of the venue, accessibility and the complexity of the production. As a general rule: allow as much time as you think you will need to carry out all the tasks, and then double it. It is far better to have a lot of extra time to deal with any unforeseen complications and omissions.

While it will be necessary for the director to be on hand for discussion about any changes that become necessary, and just to ensure that there have been no misunderstandings, the get-in should be under the general supervision of the stage manager. All bits of the set should have been gathered together before the get-in, and the stagehands and crew instructed in their tasks. The get-in should basically be a process of assembly, putting all the bits of the set into place, and fitting all the lights and sound equipment. If there is any last-minute painting and decorating to be done, which cannot be carried out until the basic set is in place, time must be allowed to ensure that it is all dry before the technical rehearsal. Crucial details for the actors must also be checked: do the doors and windows open the right way (onto or off the set), and on which sides are they hinged? Which items need to be firmly fixed, and which must be moveable?

One must also think about the audience at such times. Are all the crucial parts of the set within their sight lines? Will any parts of the set mask any of the actors at crucial moments? Hence the presence of the director is important. Usually, if there has been good planning, this will be a very boring occasion for the director, with nothing really to do, unless he/she is willing to lend a hand. Once a good working relationship has been established in the group between the director and the stage manager, it will be possible to leave the entire get-in in the hands of the stage manager.

One very important responsibility of the stage manager is making sure that all the safety guidelines are adhered to. These can be itemised as follows:

- Make sure that there is sufficient lighting backstage to facilitate access for all cast and crew.
- Leave no unguarded sharp edges on any parts of the scenery or other objects on the set or in access routes to the set.
- Leave no unplaned wooden surfaces where cast or crew are likely to put a hand or which they may otherwise come into contact with.
- Tape down all cables, wires and ropes, especially all those running over the floor in the backstage area and in access routes to the stage.
- The edges of all steps and raised edges of the set and the edges of rostra, etc, which are not in the area of the set visible to the audience, should be taped with luminous or at least bright tape (white or yellow), to make them clearly visible in semi-darkness.
- All objects suspended over the set or the backstage area should be checked to make sure that they are securely fixed. This includes items of scenery to be flown, candelabra, counterweights, etc.
- There should be no naked fire or items such as lit cigarettes or candles anywhere in the backstage area. If the text specifies their inclusion onstage, the possibilities for substitute effects should be explored. Such items should at all times be under the direct supervision of the stage manager, and the current legal requirements regarding fire hazards for the building should be checked.
- All bolts and metal joints and supports should be made secure and checked regularly.
- Check that no member of the cast or crew is expected to stand in an area where a curtain or an item of scenery, etc, is to be lowered.

THE TECHNICAL REHEARSAL

Keeping strictly to certain priorities is crucial for a successful technical rehearsal. No technical rehearsal runs without hitches and problems because, while one wants things to run as smoothly as possible, one of the important functions of such a rehearsal is precisely to discover such hitches and problems and fix them before it is too late. Broadly speaking the priority is: technicalities before acting. Every single technical aspect of the production must be checked and double-checked and sequences run through again (and yet again) if they do not run well the first time. In order to focus on the checking of technical cues above all, large chunks of the play are often omitted, jumping from one technical cue to a suitable point before the next. This may annoy and frustrate the actors, making them feel a lot like puppets, but all of them should be warned of this in advance. If there has to be a delay while something technical is fixed (the angle of a light, the timing of a sound cue, etc), it may be possible to let the actors carry on with their scene for a while, but as soon as the stage manager is ready for the next cue, they will have to be interrupted. For the stage manager is God at the technical rehearsal. The director may have to do a lot of soothing of tempers!

If the production includes a musical director and/or choreographer they too will have to be prepared to submit to the priorities of the stage manager, though, since their work also involves some technical aspects (musical cues and the like), they should not hesitate to ask the stage manager to run a sequence again, so that they can practise coming in on the cues.

Omitting some chunks of the play does not necessarily mean that the technical rehearsal will be shorter than a normal complete run-through. In fact it usually takes much longer, because there will be many pauses for checks, repeats and other delays. The rehearsal must continue quite simply until *all* the technical cues have been checked, and cast and crew should be told that they will be expected to stay on this occasion till after midnight if necessary! Arrangements should be made in advance for getting home late. The pauses for checks are all part of the usual procedure of a technical rehearsal. No one need feel dismayed at the prospect, nor despair that the play will ever be ready for performance. When things seem to be dragging and you begin to wonder why you bothered to come, it should be remembered that everyone's presence is crucial on this occasion. An actor playing a bit part may provide a crucial cue for lighting or sound. Also cues take various forms: a cue can be a few lines of text (it is therefore important to get cue lines in the right order and in the right place!); it can be an action (someone gets up from a chair, picks up a phone, turns left, turns right, etc); it can be another special effect (the door bell rings, followed by a flash of lightning, or, after a gunshot, sudden music is heard, etc). It must be remembered at all times that it will definitely *not* be alright on the night if all cues are not run several times to ensure that the transitions are smooth and that there are no delays. Delays can cause unwanted laughter in the audience at dramatic moments (an actor turns off a light switch and not until five seconds later does the lighting change, for example).

Nowadays, lighting and sound cues can all be plotted on comput- erised switchboards. Intensity, frequency and length of time can all be programmed in, so that all it needs is an instruction over the intercom – usually placed just offstage left or right – from the stage manager to the lighting or sound boxes for the person responsible to click on the next cue. If the production facilities are more primitive, it will still require a signal from the stage manager to the person operating the lights or the sound to bring in the effect on cue. It is normal, and indeed wise, for the stage manager to give a warning in advance that a technical cue is due, with a reminder of the nature of the cue, just to be doubly sure that there are no misunderstandings.

The best position for the stage manager's desk, with room for 'the book', a lamp and intercom system, must be where he/she can have a good overall view of the set, both onstage and backstage, as well as communicate with everybody involved: in the dressing rooms, green room and lighting and sound boxes (if available), at the opposite side of the stage where there may be stagehands, and with the musical director, if relevant. This usually proves to be just off downstage left or right, in the wings. The reason for the stage manager having as good a view of the performance as possible is that there are other cues which he/she has to supervise relating to the set itself: the removing and placing of objects between scenes, the shifting of scenery, etc. The SM also has to decide when the curtains (known as the tabs, which is short for tableau curtains) have to be opened or closed.

Another thing which actors can do while various technical problems are being sorted out is have someone at the back of the auditorium check for voice projection. The occasion also gives them a chance to try out their make-up in the stage lighting, and get second opinions from people in the auditorium.

It should also be remembered that 'technical' implies all physical movements and actions on the stage, so that the actor should check that all steps he/she has to climb are accessible and in the expected place, and can be managed in the light available; that all mechanical things are working, like door knobs, switches, kitchen equipment; and that he/she can hear the verbal cues of fellow actors needed in order to time their own entrances, etc. If an actor onstage turns the other way when delivering a line, the actor offstage waiting to come on may not hear that vital cue. You may have to change your voice cue to a visual one, etc.

The curtain

Finally, this is the occasion when all the actors should practise the 'curtain' for the first time: how they will bow to the audience at the end of the play, and in what sequence they will come on to the stage to do it. It is best not to overdo things! Nothing is so tiresome as a group of actors trying to milk it for all the applause they can get. The director will have to rehearse this sequence precisely as with any other movement sequence in the play, because a ragged curtain provides a poor ending to a play. The usual convention is for the actors to come on in pairs, starting with the minor roles, building up to the leading actors, and spreading out gradually in a line across the stage with the leads in the centre. When bowing, all actors should take their cue from one of the leading actors (having agreed beforehand who it will be). Three bows should be the maximum if it is not to look too self-indulgent. Variations are possible depending on the play, so that dancing and singing may be incorporated in the final curtain, if relevant. Final departure from the stage should be accomplished in an orderly, practised fashion, with reasonable distances being kept between each person. Nothing creates such a bad image at the end of a play as a group of actors jostling each other to get offstage.

THE DRESS REHEARSAL

A simple definition of a dress rehearsal is that it should be exactly like the first night, but without the audience. In fact a small invited audience should be encouraged: friends, family, any keen acquaintances of cast or crew, especially any who have not attended any previous rehearsals and are seeing it all for the first time. Actors need an audience and performances tend to lift and move into top gear when an audience is present. It is useful for any play, but especially for a comedy, to help the actors with their timing, and indicate where one can expect laughs and where not. In my own experience as an actor I have never felt I was giving it my all until I knew that an audience was attending to every word I uttered. One may be able to give a good performance at a dress rehearsal, but for many actors, all the stops are only really pulled out when there is a large paying audience out there expecting to be entertained.

It is wise to arrive as early as possible for a dress rehearsal, in order to get into costume and put make-up on well in advance. Once you get into a routine during performances you may be able to cut it a little more finely. The dress rehearsal is also the last chance you as an actor may get to see the rest of the play as the audience will see it, so many actors like to sit in the auditorium when they are not due onstage for some time. It is also the best opportunity for photographs. It can be arranged for these to be taken during the actual dress rehearsal performance, in the interval (you will need a break as in a real performance), or after the rehearsal is over.

Directors will vary in their preference for giving notes and comments after the dress rehearsal. Some may be necessary, but as well as pointing out any glaring errors, this is also a time above all for encouragement and boosting of morale. Actors may also welcome a last chance to ask the director if certain sequences went well.

Even at a dress rehearsal there can be hitches and problems, and one should not despair if they occur. Think of it in a positive light: it is good that you noticed them in time. Also, actors will occasionally forget their lines and have to recover themselves and soldier on. I have already stated in the section on prompting that I prefer an actor to press on and make up their own words in character, rather than drop out of character and call for a prompt. If you continue convincingly during an actual performance, the chances are that the audience will not even notice that lines have been changed or omitted. Most of them will not know what you should have been saying anyway.

3. THE RUN

THE FIRST NIGHT

There is in the theatre the tradition of the actor being backstage by 'the half', the half hour before curtain-up. Any amateur actor of some experience will be in the dressing room well before that, especially on the first night. It will hopefully have been possible to practise using the dressing room facilities by the technical rehearsal at least, but possibly not under the most favourable conditions. In any case, it is best not to take chances. Unless one is a very experienced actor it is not possible to judge exactly how much time one will need to get into costume and put on make-up. The timing of one's arrival is especially important if one is a 'beginner', an actor who has to appear in the first scene. By the second or third performance one can usually gauge how much time one needs, and things start to settle into a routine.

There is a pleasant tradition in many drama groups, professional or amateur, of actors sending each other cards and/or bunches of flowers, and also of other members of the crew, or people closely associated with the production, sending some such tokens to the actors and also to the director. Sometimes these gifts are addressed to the cast and crew as a whole. Actors need constant reassurance and it is a tradition worth maintaining, one of its functions being to reinforce the sense of interdependence that the best productions acquire, the feeling of all being in it together and needing to support each other. Finding such gifts waiting for them on their dressing table can be especially reassuring to new recruits and inexperienced actors.

By the first night virtually all the director's work is done. His or her presence is, however, still important, not quite in the same way as with the conductor of an orchestra or the captain of a ship perhaps, but a little like a sports coach, who cannot join in the game, but should be there to bolster confidence before and during the match. Unlike many a sports coach, however, aggressive pep-talk is out. Actors do not want to hear at this stage about any last-minute changes, or weaknesses that should be overcome. More power to their elbows is what is needed. For the director just to be there and chat warmly and encouragingly is enough. I once directed a two-handed, one-act play by Strindberg, and just before curtain up I sought out the two actresses who were waiting nervously in the wings. I mumbled something like, 'I'm out front with you all the way.' One of the actresses told me after the performance that it was just what they needed at that moment. It gave them that little bit of extra strength. For the rest of the evening there are just three words for the director to remember in handling cast and crew: reassurance, reassurance and reassurance.

From the actors' point of view there can be a few unsettling aspects to the first night. One of these, and a dominant one, is the unpredictability of audience response. One of the most disconcerting things to have to deal with, especially for an inexperienced actor, is the unexpected laugh. It is often not only the occasion on which it occurs that is unexpected but its nature. There are laughs and laughs, and audiences have an extensive range of them: the scarcely perceptive murmur of amusement, the light, embarrassed ripple, the titter, the amazed outburst and many other shades of mirth up to the uncontrolled guffaw. Even in a comedy they do not always occur when you expect them to, nor in the manner you expect. Some sequences in the play may seem to be certain to cause sure-fire belly laughs during rehearsals but only raise mild amusement in performance. Laughs also occur on occasions when you least expect them to, and in serious plays as well, causing the actor to wonder what he/she has done wrong. It must be remembered that the audience sees the broader picture and, experiencing the play for the first time, often notices things which may not have been obvious in rehearsals. Never try to analyse where the laugh came from, just be thankful for it. When I was acting in a Shakespeare play once I got a great laugh on one of my lines, but when I strove consciously to attract it in subsequent performances it never came... until I completely forgot about it and let it come naturally again.

Not only in the case of laughs, but also in relation to other aspects of performance, the audience can help a lot with timing: just knowing that they are watching helps an actor to sense how long to hold a reaction, how far to go in revealing their feelings, etc. A small, intimate audience of acquaintances at the dress rehearsal may have revealed much, but it takes a full audience of complete strangers to enable an actor to complete their performance.

If an actor gets a warm, encouraging response from the audience, however, it is crucial for them not to rise to the bait and seek more. They should continue to perform as rehearsed, without striving for effect. If they risk going over the top, it may not work, and the performance will lose authenticity.

Some directors like to give feedback at the end of every performance, but in my experience actors do not welcome it. Comments only need to be made to individuals after the show if something critical has gone wrong. By this stage most actors are very much aware of what they did well and what did not work, and why it did not. On the other hand, the director should always be ready to respond if an actor seeks advice on something.

DURING THE RUN

In all runs of plays, whether they be short or long, the quality of the performances will vary, both of individual actors and of the cast as a whole. It often happens that the second night feels a little flat after the euphoria of discovering that it all actually works on the first night. You expect wonders, that the performance will rise to even greater heights, but this may not happen. Also, while one actor's performance may seem less energetic than on the first night, another's may well be very much on the ball. The pace may seem too fast or too slow compared with the first night. The audience may respond completely differently. When an actor feels confident, their actual performance may seem to them to be just average in retrospect, while when they feel lacking in energy and inspiration, they may turn in their best performance of the run. If you have a Friday night performance you may experience one of two extreme conditions: the audience may feel so weary at the end of the week that they take in everything in a very mindless way and seem to be dull, missing the points and the laughs; on the other hand it may be crying out to be amused and be willing to laugh at almost anything. The size of the audience will also affect the general atmosphere. A small audience is more self-conscious and reluctant to reveal its feelings; a large audience is more ready to let itself go. Whatever happens, the actors must not let an audience distract them from the qualities of the performance which they have worked hard to produce. Otherwise the production will become somewhat lax and self-indulgent. This is above all what the director must look out for during the run and warn the actors about if necessary.

For the actors, it is also important to go back to the text daily to check that they are delivering the correct lines. It is so easy to get into bad habits and errors, and ad libs can come to seem to be part of the original, when they are not.

THE LAST NIGHT

A dangerous thought occurs to many actors on the last night. This is what may be dubbed the 'Last Chance Syndrome'! It is the last time to get it right, to get that laugh, to milk the play for what it is worth. The result can be that the last performance is actually the worst. All actors move about the stage with the thought at the back of their minds that it is the last time they will utter those words in that place in that way to a live audience. This awareness can lead to relishing the details too much and losing sight of the overall structure and rhythm of the play. It is best to try and cultivate, if possible, a feeling of its being just another performance, and for everyone to pay attention to the job in hand as they have done hitherto.

At the end of the performance things are far from over. There is the get-out to face before you can go off and celebrate with a last-night party.

THE GET-OUT

It is rare that the management of a venue will allow you an extra day just for the purposes of dismantling and removing all your set and equipment. If you are in that fortunate situation, however, the get-out can be undertaken the morning after. Everything can be left and locked up on the last night and sorted out the next morning. There is, however, much to be said for having the get-out on the last night, because then there is a real sense of completion shared by all the people concerned, cast and crew mucking in together to help get everything out and stowed away. Then everybody can truly celebrate together. Nothing puts a damper on a party so much as a large number of the guests having to get up early the next day to undertake the tiring manual labour of the get-out. With everybody pitching in, things also get sorted out sooner.

Getting out also does not take half as long as getting in; you don't have to double-check everything. You do, however, need to be aware of safety issues: do not remove supports until the superstructure has been safely dismantled, etc. The get-out also needs to be planned in advance (again the province of the stage manager), to ensure that everyone knows where everything should go. The props assistant must supervise the return of all props to their rightful owners; costumes may have to be packed and returned to the hire company; items of set, props and clothing that can be re-used in a future production must be put into suitable storage, or at least stored somewhere for the night, until such storage can be arranged. Lighting and sound equipment has to be dismantled under the supervision of capable experts and returned whence it came. Finally, the stage and dressing rooms have to be swept clean. It is the least courtesy that should be shown to the management, if one wants to use the venue again.

THE LAST-NIGHT PARTY

Every production wants and needs a last-night party. It rounds off the whole enterprise in celebratory fashion and allows all involved to wind down and prepare to face the dullness of everyday life again. It is a parting of sweet sorrow indeed. It is also a chance to express gratitude to all who have participated. Future plans and hopes can also be aired. One can look back, too, at all those amusing and crazy moments during rehearsals and performances, relishing it all while the memories are fresh.

A basic question concerning the last-night party is: who is going to orga-nise it? Most of the cast and crew will be too busy during the run in the theatre to have any time to think of such things. However, one or two of the crew may be able to consider taking on the task. If there is a director's assistant, for example, his or her duties will have been mainly fulfilled by the first night. The persons responsible for organising publicity could also lend a hand. Quite often spouses, partners and friends of the actors and other crew are willing to take on the task of preparing food and drink and finding a suitable venue. While some may prefer to have the party in the theatre and actually on the stage, this may not be the best arrangement, especially if you have to vacate the building by a specified time. Also, having cleared up after the production, it will not be a pleasant task to have to clear up after the party as well before going home. In my experience it is far better to agree on using a group member's house for the occasion. People can take it in turns from one production to the next, and this also has the advantage that those who volunteer to organise it can get everything set up while the rest of the cast and crew are helping with the get-out. It also means that, if the hosts are willing, the party can go on for as long as desired: many a last-night party can last into the small hours.

For the sake of the general morale and spirit of the group, there are a number of things worth arranging for such a party, and also some that should be avoided:

The DOs

- Do organise the buying of gifts and have greetings cards signed by all the cast and crew for people who have had special responsibilities and taken on onerous tasks during the production. Apart from any other individuals who have made exceptional contributions, do not forget on any account: the director, director's assistant, stage manager, wardrobe supervisor, props supervisor, musical director and choreographer (if relevant), set designer, sound and lighting operators, prompter (if you have used one), etc. At some stage in the party, when it is felt that everybody who said they were coming has come, presentations can take place, with the usual calls for 'Speech!' when the gifts and cards are handed over. It is a good idea to leave the director till last, ceding to them the place of honour, as they will probably want to say something in general to all the company. As a director I often want to show gratitude in a personal way to certain helpers.

- Do invite to the party all spouses, partners and friends of all those who have taken part in the production, because they have had to live with it intruding into their lives for several months too.
- Do invite all people who have shown some interest in joining the group, so that they can get to know everyone in an informal way. It might be the turning point which makes them realise that this is the group for them. Remember that the need for a sense of community and social contacts is often a strong motivation for joining a drama group.
- Do make sure a special thanks is said and a special gift provided for the people who have provided their house for the party.
- Do announce or remind people of future events, and the next activity planned. This is not only useful for any newcomers you have invited but also for all involved in the production, because there is always a sense of a great void in one's life when a production is over. It is good to have something new to look forward to in the not-too-distant future: ideally auditioning for the next production, or at least a read-through of a likely play.

The DON'Ts

- Don't encourage people to drink too much and get out of control! Insensitive and thoughtless things may be said, and you will all want to work with each other again.
- Don't take the opportunity to analyse the weaknesses in your production, what could have been improved, where you failed, etc. This may be useful on some future occasion, at a committee meeting, etc, but the last-night party is an occasion for celebration, for patting on the back, for encouraging and rejoicing that you pulled the whole thing off. It finally was alright on the night!
- Don't forget to bring a camera to take photos of everybody enjoying themselves and of the presentations, not just for your own memories, but to show prospective members what good times you have.

4. SPECIAL CONSIDERATIONS

PLAYS WITHOUT SCRIPTS

It may sound highly ambitious for an amateur group to consider undertaking the performance of a play without a script, and indeed many of the actors themselves may be extremely nervous of doing so. Once a group has become established, however, and if there are a number of willing members keen to experiment, it is worth considering seriously. I have undertaken several such productions with groups of students, with very impressive results, and now feel confident that any group of enthusiastic and imaginative amateurs can undertake such a task.

In fact, describing the procedure as producing a play without a script is something of a misnomer, because although one starts without a script one usually ends up with fairly fixed dialogue. The difference between this activity and performing a play already written is that the actors can develop their own storyline, characters and dialogue. In the cases which I supervised as director, I never suggested that the dialogue should be written down: it was the actors themselves who decided to do this once they had reached a stage of development where it seemed that the scenes were sufficiently well formed. The purpose in recording the dialogue was very much so that they could remember what they had agreed on.

It is also a reassuring aspect of such dramas – and one that can be drawn to the attention of nervous actors – that, while it is obviously important for them not to change cue lines or the sequences of argument, it is not necessary for them to repeat a speech word for word as they did in a previous rehearsal. It is their play, and unless they reveal their uncertainty through hesitation, the audience will not suspect that anything has been changed or is in any way wrong. Many actors become quite skilled at the art of ad libbing in this way.

The actors can also choose themes, ideas and situations which are of special interest to them, topical, or of local interest, perhaps dealing with some social problem or historical event. If no ideas are at first forthcoming, a brainstorming session will almost certainly throw up some rewarding ideas. All one needs is a comfortable room and a board on which to write the ideas as they come up. At first it is a good idea not to reject any idea as unworkable. Write down all ideas, even the weirdest. If the ideas are vague, press the person who suggested it to make the suggestion more specific: what would happen, how one might develop it, etc. Apart from serious topics, comic ones can be encouraged, and parodies are a rich source of creative ideas: of currently popular films and TV programmes (such as soap operas), novels, etc. The reworking of traditional stories in modern guise can also be very effective, especially as you already have a narrative structure to play with, e.g. *Romeo and Juliet*, *Hamlet* and other Shakespeare stories, or folk-tale motifs such as *Snow White*, *The Little Mermaid*, *Aladdin*, etc.

In establishing a storyline one should aim for the bare minimum in the first instance: a basic outline of what happens in each scene, little more than how it starts, the main points to be conveyed, and how it ends (though the latter point is not so crucial at this stage). The first version of the first scene for one such play I directed started with nothing more than the following note: 'Workers demonstrate against working conditions, etc. TV interviews with the workers and then with the manager of the factory. Raising basic issues.' The whole play can be outlined, scene for scene, in this fashion.

One of the things to discourage is any non-dramatic developments of the storyline. Some inexperienced actors may make suggestions such as the following: 'I think we should start by describing the characters' or 'I think we need a narrator to explain to people what we are trying to do', etc. Character should emerge from performance, what they are trying to do should be obvious from what they actually do, and the general situation must be deduced from the particular incident. Sometimes a narrator is a good and effective device, but not just to tell the story. He/she is better employed to facilitate estrangement, in the Brechtian sense, entering into a conspiratorial relationship with the audience, suggesting different ways of judging events or other possible courses of action.

There are some general principles in developing a good dramatic storyline which the actors can be reminded of to aid them in working out good ideas:

- Each scene should have a clear and interesting development (the familiar 'beginning, middle and end').
- All questions need not be answered (or even posed) at an early stage. Indeed it is better to leave the audience guessing and wondering what will happen next.
- Some kind of conflict or conflicts, issues of concern, or an event with unforeseen consequences should be established early in the drama. Resolution should be delayed and even impeded in each subsequent scene. Further complications can also be added. This is relevant to comedy as well as to serious drama.
- Establishment of character, relationships and issues should be accomplished naturally during performance through actions and words and require no artificial exposition.
- There should be a sufficient number of roles for everyone to have an interesting part to play.
- Make sure that once a character is introduced they are not forgotten about and have some meaningful role to play in subsequent scenes. This makes for coherence, interest and significance. It is possible to have a character appear in one scene only, if the play requires this, but in that case develop it as an interesting cameo performance, to ensure that the actor has something worthwhile to work on. No actor should feel that their role is unimportant.
- Do not allow a few characters to dominate the story entirely. Developing parallel but related plots which interact and are resolved together is one way to avoid this.
- If suitable for the theme of the play consider from the start ways in which to utilise individual actors' special talents, such as singing, playing music, dancing or acrobatic skills. This can add an enjoyable dimension to the production.

The amount of rehearsal time devoted to such a production need not be any longer than for a normal play, and certainly a tight rehearsal schedule should be established as for any other production. In all other respects, other than that the actors are developing their own dialogue, the production should be the same as for a scripted play. Once the basic plot outline is established, a rehearsal schedule can be drawn up in the normal way, specifying which actors are needed at which times, with the proviso that arrangements may have to be changed if any scenes undergo radical re-thinking. But if you have established a good and well-thought out storyline, this should not be necessary. Scheduling some blank rehearsals on a regular basis, say once a fortnight, would be a good idea, in case you wish to work on some scenes more thoroughly or even introduce an extra scene. It will in any case be reassuring to have such built-in flexibility, should you need it. There must be a point in the schedule, however, determined by the director, after which there will be no more changes. Actors must henceforth work on perfecting what has been agreed on, without introducing any more changes or additions. This is crucial for the work of the stage manager and all backstage crew. From then on strict observance of all priorities for a normal production must be observed. Otherwise you will never achieve a polished product.

SCHOOL PRODUCTIONS

Producing plays in schools is a specialist activity and teachers considering undertaking them will usually have had relevant training. Many schools will have a long tradition of doing an annual play production, and many teachers will already be incorporating drama activities in their normal classes in various ways, to aid comprehension in a large variety of fields, not just in the study of literature but also of history, environmental issues, ethical problems, and even science and mathematics. There is no scope in the present book to provide a detailed introduction to this topic, and those interested in undertaking drama activities and productions with school children are advised to consult the relevant studies in the field and seek advice from other experienced teachers.

While many of the technical problems in mounting a school play production will be similar to those encountered in an adult amateur group, the ways of handling the rehearsals and encouraging good performances from the children will be different. Also it can be argued that taking part is pedagogically more important than achieving good performances.

Nowadays there are also many considerations concerning the protection and safety of minors which have to be taken into account. An old friend of mine who teaches drama and movement in a school in the Brighton area has reminded me that for any activities out of school hours, such as drama rehearsals, letters of permission have to be obtained from parents, who must be duly informed of all that is required of their children during the production. ·

All arrangements for rehearsing and staging will also be very much influenced by the requirements of the school curricula, and the budget allowed by the school, etc.

Concerning the choice of plays for children to act in, there are many specially written with various age groups in mind, and it is also worth considering the possibility of having the children write their own play or even develop one without a script.

PRODUCING IN THE OPEN AIR

Most of what has been written about producing a play in this book is applicable to outdoor productions. There are obviously, however, certain aspects of an outdoor production which require special attention.

Location

Finding a suitable venue and arranging to use it may obviously present very special difficulties in the case of outdoor productions. All the normal considerations apply, as outlined earlier in relation to indoor productions: there must be suitable facilities for costume changes, toilets, access at necessary times, a practical stage area, etc. In addition, however, it should be an attractive venue which people will want to come to: you will not be able to sell many tickets if the play is performed in a backyard or on someone's allotment garden! It means scouting around in your district for attractive locations which also have a suitable space in which a production can be mounted.

Many successful open-air productions have been mounted in ancient ruins: abbeys, churches and castles. Old Sarum near Salisbury has seen many open-air productions in its time. Such locations also provide ready-made sets for the plays: romantic broken walls, battlements, stone staircases, etc. Having found a location which fires the imagination, approaches must be made to the authorities responsible for the upkeep of the property. This could be a local authority, a church, or one of the national heritage organisations such as the National Trust. If approaching such an influential body it is best to have a lot of impressive paperwork outlining your plans and requirements, as well as details of your budgeting arrangements.

Before arranging for permission to use the site, however, you must be very sure indeed that it fulfils all your requirements.

The weather

In choosing your location consideration must be given to what procedures to adopt in the case of unexpected bad weather. If the weather turns wet and windy before the start of a performance, you can just cancel the performance and offer to return the audience's money or give them tickets for another performance. If the weather takes a turn for the worse during a performance, you can make similar offers to spectators. Another solution is to make an arrangement with a nearby indoor location, to which the whole production, together with its audience, could be quickly transferred in the event of a sudden downpour. This avoids causing too much disappointment to the audience and even gets them on your side: they will be suitably impressed by your commitment. This will require at least one run-through of the play in the alternative venue and some basic lighting and sound equipment to be available. I have seen such arrangements work very well on two occasions: once with an open-air production of Schiller's *Don Carlos* in a monastery in Germany, which transferred to a nearby hall, and on another occasion with a Shakespeare production in the grounds of an abbey in the south of England, which had to transfer to the local church hall after about two acts.

Another option is to provide some sort of cover for both actors and audience, such as a large canopy, but this may involve you in considerable expense. Alternatively you could issue everyone, actors and audience, with disposable raincoats and transparent umbrellas and just soldier on!

Performance area

Some sites may offer more than one possible performance area. It may thus be possible to combine several locations, varying the sets without the need to build scenery. In good outdoor locations all one needs is usually some good props and discreetly placed curtains and drapes. It is important, however, to ensure that the performance area is not overlooked easily from outside the audience seating area. Otherwise people will not bother to pay to come in, but will stand around outside looking in. Two important concerns are how your preferred performance area is related to the audience seating area, and where a suitable location for dressing rooms might be.

Audience seating

For the audience seating, sight lines and whether there is a natural rake are important. In theatrical terms a rake is a slope rising away from the stage, so that people behind can see over the heads of those in front. It is advisable to organise some kind of basic seating, such as fold-up chairs or stools, for at least one part of the audience. It is possible to charge a little extra for the use of these. Many drama groups like to leave large areas in which the audience can settle on the grass with their own blankets and cushions, and one I know encourages its audiences to bring picnic baskets. But the success of such an arrangement clearly depends on good weather. Even though it might be bright and dry on the day of the performance, if it has been raining the night before, sitting on damp grass will not be an inviting option. Borrowing large numbers of chairs need not be an expensive enterprise, and may even be managed free of charge. A local church or school may be willing to lend a supply of old fold-up chairs.

Dressing rooms

The dressing rooms need not be rooms as such. An area which can be curtained off from public view or where a small marquee can be erected will be adequate, provided it can be subdivided into male and female dressing rooms. Toilet facilities should also not be too far away. And very important will be the ease with which actors can move from the dressing area to access points to the performing area without being seen by the audience.

Lighting and sound

For both lighting and sound it will most probably be necessary to fix up special scaffolding on which to mount the lights and speakers. Also, a covered area should be provided for the lighting and sound operators (covered, of course, to avoid dangerous shorting, if it should rain). Lighting may not be necessary if the performances are to be matinees or late-afternoon performances on summer evenings, but if there are to be evening performances, even on summer evenings, lighting will have be brought into play as the evening darkens. This usually involves a slow raising of the brightness level.

Refreshments

Unless the venue has a nearby cafeteria, the group itself will have to lay on some kind of light refreshments for the audience in the intervals. A trestle table in a convenient corner should suffice. Check with the proprietors if the venue has a licence and current legal requirements if you wish to serve alcoholic beverages.

Acting in the open air

Acting in the open air requires some modifications to technique. For one thing, there may be much larger distances to cover on entrances and exits, and actors will have to time themselves suitably. Voice projection is problematic because, unless the performance is taking place within the confines of a ruined abbey, and the actors are surrounded by high walls, voices will be lost in the distance. Speeches uttered at one part of the audience may not be heard by the other half. There is no way of avoiding this unless one resorts to the rather awkward and unnatural adoption of body microphones. Actors must just be sure to speak loudly, clearly and slowly at all times, to ensure that the maximum number of people can hear them. There is little room for subtle acting in the open air. Facial expressions and gestures have to be bold, clear and unambiguous. Striding is usually more effective than walking. It is also often more difficult to avoid masking fellow actors in the open air than on a stage, especially if the audience is ranged around the performance area in a semi-circle.

Choosing a play

Not all plays are suitable for performance in the open air, some of them for technical reasons and others because they simply will not attract audiences to an open-air venue. Most audiences will expect some kind of spectacle, attractive costumes and special effects, as well as the charm of the venue itself. A Beckett or Pinter play is unlikely to pull them in. Shakespeare plays, with their frequent changes of scene, work well, as do Restoration comedies and farces which do not depend on too many opening and closing doors. Literary adaptations may or may not work, depending on how well they are written. To be effective, open-air productions need a lot of scenes with large groups of people moving around, providing the opportunity for spectacle. Only the occasional intimate tête-à-tête will work. While works of Jane Austen adapted for the stage will provide lots of opportunity for impressive costumes, therefore, it will be difficult to convey all those beautiful ironies with any subtlety in the open air. And do not even think of arranging dance sequences on a grass surface!

PRODUCING SHAKESPEARE

It is arguable that every play is in some way unique and requires a style of production tailored to its special characteristics. The well-turned phrases of Noël Coward or Oscar Wilde do seem to be most at home in slightly stylised productions. While many amateur actors may be willing to have a go at a Coward or a Wilde, however, inexperienced ones may be daunted by the prospect of taking on a Shakespeare. It is a pity, because once you have actually worked out what the language means and developed some feel for the rhythms, his plays are no more difficult to perform than any other period pieces. It is not necessary to have a perfect grasp of verse structure to give a convincing and creditable performance in a Shakespeare play. The most important thing for actors is to study their roles carefully, with a good annotated edition, and make sure that they understand the essence of what they are saying. Some obscurities may remain. But if they keep in their minds what a speech basically means, and speak with the conviction that they know what they are talking about, the pauses and punctuation will take care of themselves. Alternatively, if they still feel at a loss over some sequences, they can take the advice of one of the most respected actors in the classic mould, Sir John Gielgud, and let the punctuation be their cue. Remembering his experiences as a young actor he wrote in his book *Acting Shakespeare*:

> I remember thinking I could not learn the lines because there were whole speeches that I did not understand, and there was no time to discuss them... But I tried to learn about punctuation and breathing. It seemed to me that if you were not quite sure of a very difficult speech in Shakespeare, and you studied the punctuation and got it right, the sense would in some way emerge... I tried to trust to the sweep of every speech, and to mark the commas and full stops and semi-colons, and if I observed these correctly, as a bad swimmer begins to trust the water, the text seemed to hold me up.[3]

PRODUCING BRECHT

Another playwright who is daunting for some is Bertolt Brecht. I asked an old friend and experienced amateur actor, Philip de Grouchy, who once acted in a Brecht play I directed, what advice he would give to someone thinking of producing a Brecht play and he said: 'Don't!' He was joking, but it reflects most people's fear of taking on one of his plays. This is a pity because many of them can be very rewarding for amateurs to undertake. For some the belief that it is necessary to study and understand his theory of 'estrangement' (*Verfremdungseffekt*) puts them off completely. Of course, one could spend hours reading up on the theory and learning about how all aspects of the production should be geared to making the audience think critically about how the play helps them to understand the contradictions and paradoxes in their own society, but doing a Brecht play is actually much more fun than the theory makes it sound. All that one basically needs to remember during the performance is the need to accentuate the ironies. It is satire, and the plays tell parables, making us all aware of how we compromise our ideals in order to survive. There is much comedy in Brecht and many of the plays include fascinating personal dilemmas. Because they are all made up of many self-contained scenes, like sequences in an epic tale, they lend themselves to convenient division for rehearsal too. As realism is not a paramount concern, many actors can double up or even play three or more roles. Emphasising the artificiality of the theatre is all part of Brecht's intention. A simple set, with uncovered lights and a few props, is all that is required for many of the plays. Although there are leading roles, the small roles are also rewarding and worth doing. Some of the plays contain music and songs which are fitted in as set pieces and easy to rehearse as separate units. An amateur drama group that wishes to do more than just entertain its audience would do well to consider trying a Brecht play.

PRODUCTIONS FOR NON-NATIVE SPEAKERS OF ENGLISH

There is much literature available providing advice for the teacher undertaking drama activities with foreign students learning English as a foreign language. The material available ranges from short books of drama games and exercises designed to teach specific grammatical points, to full-blown academic studies justifying the use of drama with evidence from research in applied linguistics. Many of the books also incorporate advice on mounting the production of plays.

The benefits of such undertakings are enormous: apart from the obvious opportunities drama provides to practise colloquial English, it also contributes greatly to building self-confidence in using the language in front of others and in interaction with others. Some schools and institutes even mount a full-scale production with an audience on a regular basis. The major differences between such productions and those of the average amateur group are the priorities: for EFL students the priorities are pedagogic; for amateurs they are aesthetic. Perfect diction and correct rendering of the text are therefore not so important as fluency and clarity of expression and meaning. For this reason also, it can be very effective to have the students write their own plays as part of the learning process, or even perform a play without written dialogue. This latter option is not as difficult as it may sound: it involves preparing summaries of each scene and of the plot as a whole, and improvising the dialogue and action for each scene with the students. With regular rehearsals, the dialogue gradually becomes fixed, but only after much experimentation.

It is also possible, of course, to combine the interests of EFL students with a passion for drama by setting up an amateur drama group devoted to producing plays with non-native speakers of English. They might enjoy setting up such groups among themselves, perhaps with a native speaker as consultant.

EXPATRIATE PRODUCTIONS

The undertaking of productions of plays among expatriate communities is fraught with its own particular difficulties. It is very difficult to give any advice which will be true for every circumstance. If productions are to be performed entirely within the expatriate community, with expatriate native speakers of English performing before an audience of expatriate native speakers of English, and within the confines of an embassy or expatriate club, the conditions and requirements are likely to be no different from performing a play in the home country. Once you start to involve local people, however, non-native speakers of English whose homes are in the country in question, all sorts of cultural factors have to be considered.

I once tried to establish such a mixed group, with the noble aim of enabling and encouraging intercultural understanding: it did not survive very long. According to the degree of difference between the cultural norms of the cultures involved, there will be all sorts of considerations to bear in mind at every stage. Not least among such considerations in many countries will be how far you can go in the depiction of intimacy on the stage. In some countries the notion of ensemble acting, with all actors helping and making suggestions in the rehearsal process, is difficult to accept: they will instead expect to be told exactly what to do by the director. Even arranging rehearsals may prove problematic in a country which has extremely long working days, and in which loyalty to company and/or family must always have priority. Some English-language drama groups have been able to survive, but it is usually those that rely heavily on expatriate members.

If there is any general word of advice which can be given it is this: get to know the culture of your host country well before even thinking about establishing a multicultural drama group.

FESTIVALS

Once an amateur drama group is established and has mounted several successful productions, some members may be tempted to suggest taking a production to a drama festival. There are now many in various parts of the country, mainly in the summer, to take advantage of the best time of year for outside performances. It is very difficult to lay down guidelines for taking a production to a festival, as each festival will have its own requirements and guidelines. A lot of reading around and scouring the Internet has to be undertaken to gain the requisite information.

Certainly there are some basic factors to consider before committing to such a venture:

- What is your basic financial outlay likely to be, including any necessary transport and accommodation costs?
- Will the festival be paying you any fee for your performance, or will you get a straight percentage of the box-office takings?

- How is publicity to be arranged?
- Is the play you are planning to take suitable and adaptable to the circumstances of the festival?
- What is the nature of your performance venue?
- What services do the festival organisers provide, and which are you expected to arrange?
- What storage facilities will there be at the festival?
- Can you get away with minimal scenery and props? How extensive a set could you actually manage?

Generally it is best to plan the production with the specific needs of the festival in mind, rather than roughly adapting a production you have already mounted in another venue.

ACTING WITH CHILDREN AND ANIMALS

Incorporating children into amateur productions where the rest of the cast and crew are adults involves a different set of considerations from producing plays where all the participants are children.

Obviously care must be taken at all times to ensure that the children are safe, both from the danger of physical injury on the set and backstage, and also from the threat of any kind of abuse. A responsible adult, either a parent or someone approved by the parents, should be on hand at all times to look after them. The most convenient solution, as I have experienced with many productions, is to have any roles for children played by the offspring of members of the cast or crew. It must also be ensured that the drama activity does not disturb their normal school work and homework. If necessary, a chat to their class teacher or head teacher in advance of final casting would be advisable, to make sure that the child's welfare and studies are taken fully into account.

There are not, to the author's knowledge, any specific regulations regarding the supervision of children in amateur performances outside the school environment, apart from those laws relating to the protection of minors in all circumstances.

In casting child actors, one should look out not only for general acting capability and suitability for the role, but a sense of responsibility and the ability to work with a group. You need to know that you can rely on the child to be present when needed and not to vary their performance at every rehearsal.

All that said, the main worry of actors working with children is that they are likely to steal the show, drawing all the audience's attention to themselves. They may also do something completely unpredictable. Among fellow adult actors patience is needed and the ability to ad lib in case of emergency!

With animals, ad libbing is not so helpful, except in cases in which it may be necessary to call an animal's name to keep it under control. If it is not possible to obtain a specially trained animal, the second choice should be an animal which is the pet of the actor in charge of it in the play. In this case there is a reasonable chance of its obeying its master or mistress. Whatever happens, make sure it is on a lead. The whole play will fall apart if it starts wandering around and investigating the set. It must be supposed that dogs are the most commonly used animals in plays and they are very inquisitive by nature.

If an animal is clearly referred to in the text and central to the plot, there is no way around it: you must include the animal somehow. Far better, however, to avoid using animals altogether if possible. Apart from stealing the show even more certainly than children, they are also far less reliable, and tend easily to revert to their natural instincts. Once, when acting as a lord in an open-air production of a Shakespeare play, I had two attendants each with a pair of hunting dogs on leashes. One of the attendants lost control of his dogs and they started leaping around and roaming off towards the audience. Fortunately I had a line coming up in which I had to instruct my attendants to 'look to my hounds'. I was able to make this line come very much alive on this occasion as we all hurried to get them under control again. In a professional production of an Ibsen play (*When We Dead Awaken*) two Afghan hounds ignored the heavy drama in progress around them and amused themselves by mating in full view of the audience. Needless to say both actors and audience were soon in hysterics. If the dog appears in a comedy it might be possible to use the old comedian's gag of using a stiff lead with a collar and an imaginary dog. In the hands of a good comedy actor it can be hilarious.

FROM AMATEUR TO PROFESSIONAL

Changing from being an amateur to a professional actor is not a decision one should make lightly. It is not just a question of being confident of your ability, but of a commitment to a whole different lifestyle. I knew an actor who had done it in middle age, but could only risk it because he was in a secure emotional relationship with someone who had agreed to support him financially until he acquired some success and was able to support himself. It is undoubtedly easier for younger people to take the risk, because if it does not work out then there is still the chance of entering another career. But becoming a professional actor also often involves undergoing professional training and acquiring the technical skills necessary to sustain the task of acting on a daily basis and not just as a hobby in one's spare time. Without evidence of suitable training or some kind of track record it will be very difficult to obtain roles in a profession in which it is common to be out of work for long periods.

For those seriously interested in making the transition, details of some leading drama schools and sources of further advice are included in the 'Resources' section at the end of this book.

Those who are interested in pursuing the technical skills necessary to embark on a career in theatrical production are best advised to consult the invaluable publication *Contacts* (see under 'Other Useful Reference Books' in the 'Resources' section). It is a good starting point for discovering information about relevant training courses and professional openings.

THE 'M' WORD AND OTHER SUPERSTITIONS

You cannot consider yourself a serious man or woman of the theatre unless you reveal some familiarity with theatre lore and show some respect for its superstitions. As some actors take the superstitions more seriously than others, it is best to play safe and avoid offending sensitivities.

Some of the superstitions have passed into general knowledge and parlance, but most people have only a vague understanding of their significance. Indeed their origins are in most cases shrouded in mystery; while there has been much speculation about them, nobody knows for sure how they arose.

The most famous superstition concerns the 'Scottish Play', as Shakespeare's play *Macbeth* must always be referred to within the confines of a theatre building. Anyone inadvertently mentioning the title of the play, or quoting from it, and especially from the witches' incantations, can only avoid the most terrible catastrophe by leaving the theatre building immediately, turning round three times, spitting, cursing and then knocking three times on the door in order to be allowed to re-enter.

Ghosts also feature prominently in theatre superstitions. Traditionally a theatre should always be closed one day a week – Sunday in the UK, Monday in the US – to allow the ghosts a chance to perform their own plays. It is also traditional to leave at least one light burning in an empty theatre, most commonly downstage centre, so that the ghosts have enough light to see their way by. This also has an obvious practical use, preventing people coming into a darkened theatre from falling over something and injuring themselves. But this could well be a rationalisation.

It is also considered bad luck for an actor to whistle, either onstage or off. This may have its origins in an old practice of stagehands giving each other coded whistles as signals. By whistling an actor might therefore confuse the backstage crew.

Perhaps the most widely known superstition is that one should not wish actors 'Good luck!' before a performance, because it is sure to bring about the opposite effect. Instead actors say to each other, 'Break a leg!', implying the opposite.

There are many other beliefs that have spread over the years, creating different degrees of anxiety in actors, according to the extent of their credulity, and they also vary from culture to culture. Perhaps it is not surprising that so many superstitions should have grown up around a profession which, historically, has always been an insecure one, fleeting in its glory.

5. RESOURCES

BOOKS REFERRED TO IN THE TEXT

Callow, Simon, *Being an Actor*, London: Penguin, 1985 (first published 1984).

Gielgud, John, *Acting Shakespeare*, London: Pan, 1997 (first published 1991).

Zucker, Carole, *In the Company of Actors*, London: A & C Black, 1999.

OTHER USEFUL BOOKS

Davies, Gill, *Create Your Own Stage Production*, London: A & C Black, 2000.

Good checklists and flow charts.

Griffiths, Trevor R, *Stagecraft*, London: Phaidon, 2004 (first published 1982).

A well-illustrated book covering all aspects of stage production. Good on explanations of technicalities, but often of more relevance to the professional than amateur stage.

Morris-Michell, Geoff, *Directing Amateur Theatre*, Plymouth: Northcote House, 1996.

Many good practical hints from the point of view of the director of amateur shows. Useful recommendations for further reading and lists of equipment suppliers.

Sharman, Helen E, *Directing Amateur Theatre*, London: A & C Black, 2004.

Good general survey of the whole production process, with a useful section of advice on festivals.

ACTORS' GAMES AND EXERCISES

Barker, Clive, *Theatre Games*, London: Methuen, 1977.
For the director and actor who really take games seriously, with an in-depth analysis of the theory and psychology of it all. The activities are buried in the text, and it is necessary to read whole chapters to find them.

Brandes, Donna, and Phillips, Howard, *Gamesters' Handbook*, Cheltenham: Stanley Thornes, 1990 (first published 1977).
A large variety of games and other activities, not only useful for actors but also for teachers of all kinds.

Brooks, Mary, *The Drama Ideas Bank*, Hemel Hempstead: KCP Publications Ltd, 2002.
Designed for use in the classroom, the book has useful activities for all ages, with many involving mime, role play and dialogue development that can be easily photocopied.

Pickering, Kenneth, *Drama Improvised*, Colwall: J Garnet Miller, 1997 (first published 1957).
The publishers describe it as a 'source book for teachers and therapists' and this indicates the dual focus of the book. Its strength lies in the imaginative suggestions for improvisation.

BOOKS ON USING DRAMA IN LANGUAGE TEACHING

Wessels, Charlyn, *Drama*, in the series 'Resource Books for Teachers', Oxford: OUP, 1987.
Practical advice for using drama techniques in English-language teaching, including many imaginative activities and recommendations for setting up drama projects.

Dougill, John, *Drama Activities for Language Learning*, London: Modern English Publications, Macmillan, 1994 (first published 1987).

ADVICE ON SELECTING PLAYS

The Guide to Selecting Plays, published by Samuel French Ltd, London, with a new updated edition every few years. This is easily the best and most comprehensive guide to plays available for amateur performance, with indexes organised on various principles, enabling the reader to find plays with very precise requirements (by number of characters, by period or type of play, by theme, and with indications of the numbers of male and female roles, etc). Up-to-date advice is also provided on copyright law and royalties. It is possible to sign up for French's mailing service and receive regular updates.

OTHER USEFUL REFERENCE BOOKS

Amateur Theatre Yearbook, by Platform Publications Ltd, annually. This directory provides much useful information on organisations of use to amateur drama groups, including, for example, marketing experts, suppliers of props and set designers, etc. Email: cvtheatre@aol.com

Contacts, a yearbook published by 'The Spotlight', London. It is described by its publishers as 'the essential handbook for everyone working or wanting to work in the entertainment industry', and has been a regular annual publication since 1947, containing over 5,000 listings, which are updated annually. It is truly the most comprehensive work of reference available on all aspects of the performing arts. There are sections with listings on a wide range of relevant organisations: agents, arts centres, arts councils, costumes, wigs and make-up, dance schools and coaches, festivals, film and video facilities and training schools, publicity and press representatives, role-play companies, set construction, lighting, sound and scenery, alternative and community theatre, children's and young people's theatre, English-speaking theatre in Europe, regional repertory, etc. There are also many articles providing advice on the range of services advertised: how to acquire an agent, opportunities for child actors with advice for parents, how to become a media presenter, becoming an extra (walk-on or supporting artists), preparing for an audition, becoming a professional dancer, choosing suitable drama training, etc. www.spotlight.com

PERIODICALS

Amateur Stage, published monthly. It contains advisory articles on make-up, lighting, sound, marketing, production and sponsorship, with reviews of new plays and surveys of developments in amateur theatre.

The Stage, published weekly. It is described as 'a weekly for the entertainment industry', and, while aimed at the professional, contains articles on acting, theatre services and media of interest and relevance to the amateur. There is also a large range of useful advertisements: for video and DVD services, theatre festivals, fringe theatre, drama schools, university drama schools, backstage jobs, auditions for both professionals and amateurs, suppliers of costumes, wigs, lighting and sound equipment, backdrops and stage sets. There is also a large section of classified small ads with items of interest to both professionals and amateurs. www.thestage.co.uk

USEFUL WEBSITES

Amateur drama in general

www.amdram.net
The website of the amateur drama community with advice on producing plays, auditions, venues, bookshops, etc.

www.amdram.co.uk
The website of an association devoted to amateur drama, with much good advice about production, etc.

Stage management

www.stagemanagementassociation.co.uk
For all matters relating to stage management, this website, serving professional stage managers, is a useful first port of call.

Make-up

www.fashion.arts.ac.uk
www.soton.ac.uk
Information concerning courses on theatrical make-up.

www.makeupeffects.co.uk
An online make-up shop.

Costume

www.wimbledon.arts.ac.uk
Information about courses on costume.

www.nationaltheatre.org.uk
www.royalexchange.co.uk
For information and advice on costume hire.

Props

www.shop4props.com
www.props4shows.co.uk
Between them these sites offer a large range of props, including fake food
and animals, etc.

Sound effects

There are many websites providing sound effects. The following are worth
checking for the variety on offer:

Free sites: www.soundswap.com
               www.stonewashed.net

To buy: www.sounddogs.com
            www.sound-effect.com

Drama festivals

www.ndfa.org.uk
The website of the National Drama Festival Association, with 50 member festivals in the UK at the last count.

Funding

www.aandb.org.uk
The website of Arts and Business (A & B), which aims to 'help business people support the arts and the arts inspire business people'. Much useful and up-to-date advice on financing in general and seeking sponsorship.

www.britishcouncil.org/arts-drama
With sound advice for obtaining financial support and funding.

Training courses

www.cssd.ac.uk
The Central School of Speech and Drama is a world-renowned school, part of the University of London, with a wide range of degree and non-degree courses related to acting and the theatre, including many short courses on such subjects as voice training, dialect and accent coaching, directing, singing, etc, as well as acting courses for those with various levels of experience.

www.lamda.org.uk
The website of the London Academy of Music and Dramatic Art. LAMDA offers regular courses of many kinds on acting, stage management, directing and stage design, with summer courses on various topics, such as Shakespeare, lighting, auditioning techniques, etc.

www.rada.org
The website of the Royal Academy of Dramatic Art. As well as providing full-time courses for would-be actors and stage managers, the organisation regularly offers short courses on a range of useful skills, including production skills and directing, as well as acting workshops.

NOTES

1 Carole Zucker, *In the Company of Actors*, A & C Black, 1999, p. 9.
2 Simon Callow, *Being an Actor*, Penguin, 1985, p. 89.
3 John Gielgud, *Acting Shakespeare*, pp. 31–2.

INDEX

ARTS REVIEWS

...and how to write them

www.kamerabooks.co.uk

INTRODUCTION

Most reviewers wake up every morning and can't believe their luck. They're getting paid to do what many of them would actually bribe someone to let them do anyway. They are going to be rewarded for indulging an obsession. Ahead of them is a day which they can devote to the activity that, with the possible exceptions of sex and food, they love best in the entire world. This they will be able to describe as their work. Truly, whoever called being a reviewer 'the world's best job' was not wrong. The role offers you an irresistible balance of passion, pleasure and lack of responsibility. And you may well get paid for it. Life doesn't get much better.

In this book I will be talking about reviewers rather than critics, although the terms mean almost the same thing. Of course the choice of word is deliberate – I'm a writer, I choose words as other people choose washing powder or life partners, for their essential qualities. Critic may be the traditional name for the person who is a professional audience for an art, but it sounds a little negative and the baggage that comes with it is heavy and ugly. I am also an artist; people talk about constructive criticism but, to the artist, the stuff in the media is rarely that. Artists do not often experience media criticism as a positive contribution to their work.

Critic is also narrow word; it doesn't suggest the central role that reviewers can play in championing, advancing, refining or popularising the art that they love. Their influence can be profound. Quentin Tarantino acknowledged his debt to the film critic of *The New Yorker*, Pauline Kael, whose notices he read faithfully while growing up, saying that she was, 'as influential as any director was in helping me develop my aesthetic'.[1]

Here is Sir Tom Stoppard explaining that when he began to write plays they were directly influenced by *The Observer*'s drama critic, Kenneth Tynan: 'Tynan mattered for his youth, his virtuosity in print, his self-assurance, his passion and above all for his self-identification with the world he wrote about. So... when I sat down to try to write a play, I was consciously trying to write for him.'[2]

Perhaps the most thrilling moments in a reviewer's life are the times when it falls to you to be a witness to history. A young soprano appeared in an obscure opera at the Olympia Theater in Athens and one of the critics who heard her, Vangelis Mangliveras, wrote, 'That new star in the Greek firmament, with a matchless depth of feeling, gave a theatrical interpretation well up to the standard of a tragic actress. With her exceptional voice with its astonishing natural fluency … she is one of those God-given talents that one can only marvel at.'' His judgment was so apt that, Maria Callas was known afterwards as 'The God-Given' even by the rivals who hated her.

A great critic, says the music reviewer Norman Lebrecht, is 'the conscience of his art'. Individual critics have left their distinct imprints on our creative life; their confident judgement and their intelligent support can define a great artistic movement and create the consensus that will recognise it. Groups of critics, brought together by the beliefs and values that they share, have deliberately steered their culture in a new direction. Even before that, great critics contribute immeasurably to the cultural life of their times, informing, challenging and stimulating their readers to a better understanding of the arts.

Many artists begin their careers as reviewers. Early in their creative lives, when they have yet to mature as practitioners, they have a passion for their field and often also a clear idea of where it should be going. The most striking example of a creative movement which began as an exercise in criticism is the cinema of France's New Wave; a handful of iconoclastic youths attacked the timid, traditionalist French films of the 1950s in a new film magazine, *Les Cahiers du Cinema* and almost instantly became the legendary directors creating a new cinematic style. As a reviewer, a developing artist becomes part of a creative profession, gains an understanding of its dynamics, meets the key players, falls in with like-minded friends and has the opportunity to issue a manifesto in every notice.

Equally, many reviewers don't cross over to the creative side, either by choice or because they're in the wrong place at the wrong time. As a young film critic, I would have liked nothing better than to become part of the British film industry, but at the time there wasn't one. True, a few movies got made; it was a phenomenon like the desert rivers of the Middle East. After a long, cruel dry spell there would be a flash flood; people would hail a new British cinematic movement and then, as with a wadi in the desert, the essentials – faith or money or tax breaks – would dry up, leaving only the name, the erosion and maybe a bleached skeleton to show where there had once been abundance.

You didn't have to be a man to work on this now-you-see-it-now-you-don't enterprise but almost all the writers, directors and technicians were male. Since the work was scarce, they were fiercely protectionist. The real action in movies was not in London, but in Hollywood, Paris, Warsaw or Rome, and I had a depressing sense of being a long way away from it. So when a desperate magazine editor offered me half a page of film reviews every month if I'd deliver a spread on television as well, it was a blessing in disguise. The British film industry probably lost the dreamiest production assistant it never had.

Having struck, as I saw it, a downright Faustian bargain and become a television reviewer, I found myself part of a golden age. Better still, few writers of any calibre in the press knew anything or cared less about this Cinderella backwater of the entertainment industry – that was the reason that my editor resorted to Mephistophelian manoeuvres. Overnight I became a media authority and in a few months I was headhunted by Fleet Street and spent the next seven years with the brightest, most creative and most exciting screen talents of the time.

It was strange to operate in the no-man's land between television and newspapers, territory that was heavily mined, full of barbed wire and shell holes, haunted by the ghosts of decent writers who had died under fire. TV was then and currently remains the dominant information medium, with 95% of the population relying on it for news coverage, a fact to which newspapers at that time were responding with dour resentment. Every year the television industry creamed off the top graduates from Oxford and Cambridge, yet the editors for whom I worked dismissed their work as lowbrow mass entertainment, unworthy of their attention and of no interest to our readers. When I thought about this attitude in relation to the significance of the industry, I felt as if my head would burst with the absurdity of it. So I went to war. Stories were my ammunition. I bombarded my editors with reportage, features, profiles and essays. Most were shot down, but gradually the section editors realised that I could deliver something halfway interesting and competently written that would plug the holes in their schedules.

I was working on an evening newspaper that had a classic problem with reader loyalty. Typically, people bought the paper only once or twice a week, on their way home from work, instead of getting it every day as the readers of morning papers tend to do. I knew, as an avid reader of the critics since my teens, that a good review needs to stand alone, meaning that it should be understandable to a reader who hadn't followed any continuing debate around its subject. So I made sure that my work always passed that test, even when I was writing the TV listings.

I also loved reviewers who brought deep erudition to popular art, like Clive James, whose TV reviews glittered with running gags based on the absurdity of *Dallas*, and Alexander Walker whose film criticism took his readers inside the live debates in the industry. Banned from studying the arts by my father, I had educated myself covertly from such erudite critics, disappearing into the recesses of school library with its hallowed copy of *The Times* or rowing upriver on summer holiday mornings to buy the Sunday newspapers. I learned of Fellini from Dilys Powell, Diaghilev from Richard Buckle and Wagner from Bernard Levin. Naturally I set out to emulate my heroes, so I pitched my work far higher than the traditional TV writer, assuming that my readers were hungry for fun and for facts, and ready for a wider perspective on a medium that they took seriously even if my editors did not.

Soon I was getting fan letters and, even more impressively, the paper was getting sales. One of the most rewarding sights of my life appeared as I sat anonymously on a commuter train watching a passenger who carefully tore my column out of the paper, placed it reverently in his wallet and threw the rest of the newspaper away when he left the carriage.

After years of writing the editor passionate memos about What The Paper Needs I was allowed to launch the first media supplement in a British newspaper. It was immensely satisfying to be the first to spot a hit new series, to understand a new cult, to promote a gifted documentary-maker, to spotlight a stunning young actor or to champion a brilliant comedy performer who just hadn't had the right break yet. The people I wrote about now run the British TV industry or else they've justly become international stars: Michael Grade, Greg Dyke, Melvyn Bragg, Jane Root, Michael Apted, Stephen Frears, Julie Walters, David Jason, Jeremy Irons.

When I got the confidence to write my first book, I found that I could draw on a reservoir of goodwill in high places. Many doors opened even before I knocked on them. My first publisher was one of my readers and actually asked my agent if I'd like to write a book for her. When I needed to approach major celebrities for interviews, their gatekeepers often reported back, in wondering tones, 'He said

'Oh, I know Celia, I like her stuff, yes, tell her I'll do it." By that stage, I also knew many of the gatekeepers and had managed to win their respect too.

Crossing over into TV would have been nice but almost impossible. You didn't have to be a man to work in the industry at that time but the overwhelming majority of the people who did were male. Or else they were at least pretty; some, indeed, were the great beauties of our day, while I had an excellent face for radio. So when the day came that I woke up and realised that I wanted more, I went back to what I knew I was good at and became a novelist and had the interesting experience of being reviewed in my turn.

I soon discovered that book reviews turned out to be a great denominator of genius; when they were reviewing, first-rate writers had always read my books attentively and understood them, even if they found it alarming that they were international bestsellers. Second-rate writers read the blurb, the first page and, sometimes, the end, but felt free to advance devastating critiques on this flimsy basis.

Reviewing doesn't have to be a vocation. It can be the first writing job you land just because you're so determined to become a journalist that you'll write anything anytime anywhere for anyone, just to get started. This is an excellent attitude and will often lead to professional success. If you don't want to become a journalist that badly, perhaps you should reconsider your career choice because you'll be competing with a large number of people who are passionate at that level.

So your first review may come your way because you're the only person in the office willing to junk your plans for the evening and trek off to some poxy fringe venue in a gang crime hotspot to review an act you've never heard of and miss the last train home, all in the cause of Art, filling up a quarter of a column in your publication, and – aha! – getting a by-line. Even before that, the ability to write a review that provokes people to read and respond can be your best chance of getting published on a fan site that's doomed to disappear three months later but will leave you a by-line when it goes.

What's a by-line? It's the line that starts with 'by' and ends with your name. It's your credit for writing a piece of journalism, the proof that someone with editorial authority has deemed you sufficiently interesting and responsible to able to advance your own opinions under your own name. 'By' plus 'your name here'. In the media, a by-line is what you need to get started. Once one editor has given you a by-line, you're in the game and others will follow.

One day, you may become the editor, giving out by-lines in your turn. One day, your name may appear on cultural essays, authoritative biographies or the credits of top-rated arts shows. One day, you may be staying up late to read the first editions of the newspapers as they come up on the Web carrying reviews of *your* own film, or *your* novel, *your* art installation or *your* groundbreaking new production of *Die Walkure*. Whichever route you choose, it starts here, with the secrets of writing a great arts review.

kamera BOOKS

ESSENTIAL READING FOR ANYONE INTERESTED IN FILM AND POPULAR CULTURE

Tackling a wide range of subjects from prominent directors, popular genres and current trends through to cult films, national cinemas and film concepts and theories. Kamera Books come complete with complementary DVDs packed with additional material, including feature films, shorts, documentaries and interviews.

Silent Cinema
Brian J. Robb

A handy guide to the art of cinema's silent years in Hollywood and across the globe.

978-1-904048-63-3 **£9.99**

Dalí, Surrealism and Cinema
Elliott H. King

This book surveys the full range of Dalí's eccentric activities with(in) the cinema.

978-1-904048-90-9 **£9.99**

East Asian Cinema
David Carter

An ideal reference work on all the major directors, with details of their films.

978-1-904048-68-8 **£9.99**

David Lynch
Colin Odell & Michelle Le Blanc

Examines Lynch's entire works, considering the themes, motifs and stories behind his incredible films.

978-1-84243-225-9 **£9.99**